EXECUTIVE EDITOR
Natalie Earnheart

CREATIVE TEAM
Jenny Doan, Natalie Earnheart, Christine Ricks,
Tyler MacBeth, Mike Brunner, Lauren Dorton,
Jennifer Dowling, Dustin Weant, Jessica Toye,
Kimberly Forman, Denise Lane, Grant Flook,
Cathleen Tripp, Robbie Petersen

EDITORS & COPYWRITERS
Nichole Spravzoff, Liz Gubernatis,
Camille Maddox, Julie Barber-Arutyunyan,
Hillary Doan Sperry, Lora Kroush

SEWIST TEAM
Jenny Doan, Natalie Earnheart, Courtenay Hughes,
Carol Henderson, Cassandra Ratliff,
Janice Richardson

PRINTING COORDINATOR
Rob Stoebener

ADDITIONAL PHOTOGRAPHY
International Quilt Museum

PRINTING SERVICES
Walsworth Print Group
803 South Missouri
Marceline, MO 64658

CONTACT US
Missouri Star Quilt Company
114 N Davis
Hamilton, MO 64644
888-571-1122
info@missouriquiltco.com

06 PRESERVING QUILTS FOR YEARS TO COME

Get behind the scenes and learn how quilts are collected, curated, and cared for at the International Quilt Museum in Lincoln, NE, and the Missouri Quilt Museum in Hamilton, MO.

42 CREATE SEWING MAGIC w/MINKI KIM

A designer for Riley Blake, Minki makes the cutest creations we've ever seen! Learn about how she began sewing and get inspired to make your own whimsical creation.

56 SPRING CLEAN YOUR SEWING SPACE

Find out what kind of quilter you are and hone in on your organizational style with a few suggestions to help you find renewed inspiration in your sewing space.

78 COMMUNITY CONNECTION

The Restorative Justice Program gives offenders the chance to grow and give back to their community by making beautiful quilts for foster children.

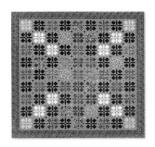

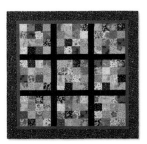

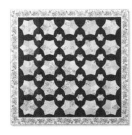
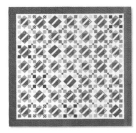

A note from Jenny

Springtime in Missouri is simply breathtaking. After the seemingly endless winter landscape with bare branches, soggy pastures, and snow drifts, finally seeing the bold little crocuses bloom in my backyard is pure bliss. Sudden thunderstorms bring torrential rain, but then there are the soft, spring mornings when sunlight streams through the split rail fences surrounding the fields and the fog slowly lifts.

Breathing in the crisp morning air and hearing the birds call outside my window always elevates my mood. One sunny morning, I'll get the urge to dislodge everything stuck in the far reaches of my quilting studio, sort out the clutter, and restore order once again after a long winter of comfort sewing. This time of renewal is filled with anticipation as I prepare myself for new ideas. And it begins in a simple way.

Organization is the start of many wonderful things. Taking the time to organize my fabrics and notions with care, lining up my thread in color order, making sure my needle is sharp and my scissors are within reach is an easy way to welcome inspiration into my life.

Taking care of your space shows love for what you have. I know it helps me appreciate everything more and I often discover a project or two I forgot about. I fall in love all over again and it fills me with a rush of fresh inspiration. And remember, your space doesn't have to be perfect for you to love it. It only has to work for you!

Jenny

JENNY DOAN
MISSOURI STAR QUILT CO.

QUILT MUSEUMS

Preserving Masterpieces for Years to Come

Museums are places where inspiration is being preserved for generations to come. When you visit a museum, it has a serene feeling, almost reverent, as people gaze on ages-old artistic creations ranging from sculptures to paintings and even quilts. Now that quilting has become recognized as an important artform in and of itself, there are museums dedicated solely to this beautiful and useful artform we love with all our hearts.

Quilts in this collection at the Missouri Quilt Museum are on loan from the National Quilt Museum in Paducah, KY. Photographed with permission.

The Missouri Quilt Museum

Like most museums, the Missouri Quilt Museum is a historical location set to celebrate the rich history of quilting. What started out as an abandoned elementary school in the middle of Quilt Town, U.S.A., has been transformed into a colorfully homespun museum with several bright rooms full of gorgeous quilts and quilting memorabilia.

So, how does a smaller quilt museum such as the Missouri Quilt Museum collect and curate quilts? At the Missouri Quilt Museum in Hamilton, MO, quilts are loaned or donated from all over the country, but they also acquire several from locals in surrounding communities and other areas in Missouri. The MQM receives several loaned quilts from The National Quilt Museum in Paducah, Kentucky, to rotate through their exhibits on a regular basis.

Though they get several loaned quilts, the MQM has an extensive permanent collection of modern quilts dating from the 1980s to the present, also from The National Quilt Museum.

The Missouri Quilt Museum receives loaned and donated quilts from all over the state and the country. After the quilts have made their arrival, they are documented as loans or donations, named, and further cataloged based on the fabrics, colors, size, pattern, features, year, maker, etc. During this process, founder and curator Dakota Redford spends time conducting research on the one-of-a-kind item and its origin before giving it a temporary home in an exhibit.
"I research in as much detail as possible each artifact that comes to the museum, often relying on the history given by the donor to get me started," Dakota said. "I like to get to know the maker and understand their passion for the art, taking into account the time in history when the person was making the quilt, their economic background, life setting, events, and circumstances. All of this helps me decide how to create an exhibit around the quilt and what details to give our guests. I like to give just enough information to get the viewer 'interested' and then let them connect with the quilter, the quilt, or its story."

The quilts donated or loaned to the Missouri Quilt Museum are given a lot of attention from the point of their arrival to the time they are removed from display. Before being placed in an exhibit, the quilts go through a photoshoot where they can enjoy the spotlight. Then, the quilt is placed in an exhibit where viewers can admire every stitch and fiber used to create the masterpiece.

Many of the masterpieces sent to this small town museum may be aged, fragile, and require special care. That's why everyone at the museum takes great care when handling, processing, and storing the quilts they are given. Some of the exhibits have signs detailing the fragility of the displayed creation so visitors know to admire without touching.

"The salt and oils that are on our skin can damage quilts significantly," Dakota said. "The staff uses gloves to handle them so as to not discolor or stain them. When not on display quilts are rolled and kept in a dark, cool space with acid-free paper and cotton to maintain their integrity. The building is temperature and humidity controlled and we use specialty lighting to ensure their protection in color and to keep them from deteriorating." As any enthusiasts would, the team at the museum safeguards all their quilts with great care.

The quilts on display are rotated every few months, so there is always something new to see. The exhibits range to present finished projects from sewing celebrities to local quilters—you may even recognize a few from Missouri Star. You can support the museum by planning a visit, getting a family or individual membership, loaning or giving quilting items to the exhibits, or donating to the elevator fund to help the museum to make this old building more accessible.

**OPEN CAMERA
SCAN CODE
VISIT
MISSOURI QUILT
MUSEUM**

A BLOCKSTAR EXHIBIT

Missouri Star's Liz Gubernatis was recently invited to show her first solo exhibit in the Missouri Quilt Museum. Nearly 20 quilts hang in the exhibit, and choosing the quilts was a challenge. Liz says, "Many of the quilts I make are for someone I love and given to them. Sometimes I couldn't part with one so I made a "matching pair" of quilts and gifted one and kept the other. It was such a trip down memory lane to collect these for display. I can see how I have grown and stretched and changed as a quilter, gaining confidence and skills, but still proud of my early efforts, too."

To learn more about how her quilt collection was selected, curated, and displayed in the museum, read the extended interview in your digital issue.

The International Quilt Museum

Pieces of quilting history are scattered throughout history museums all across the world, but a few museums have stepped up and made quilting their primary focus. The largest of these is the International Quilting Museum, located in Lincoln, Nebraska. Founded in 1997 as the International Quilt Study Center at the University of Nebraska-Lincoln, the IQM has been collecting quilts from across the world and throughout history for research, preservation, and public display. Today, they have nearly six thousand quilts ranging from simple patchwork quilts made to keep people warm to extravagant art pieces at the pinnacle of fiber arts. It contains artifacts from more than 65 countries dating back to the Middle Ages. Their goal is "to collect and exhibit works that represent quilts and quiltmaking traditions from around the world and throughout history."

The International Quilt Museum, began with a donation of 1,000 quilts. Initially, this impressive collection was housed on the University campus and it was used to create exhibits for galleries on campus and even around the world. Within a decade, the collection was moved to a brand new building complete with state-of-the-art textiles storage and three galleries made especially for exhibiting quilts. Even the architecture is a metaphor for the quilts themselves with expansive glass windows featuring linear metal bars that look like stitches representing the front of the quilt, the galleries representing the batting, and the office spaces in back representing the backing. Additionally, the reception hall is shaped like the eye of a needle. It's a clever design that quilters can truly appreciate.

Preserving their treasured pieces of quilted art begins with each new acquisition. When quilts arrive, they are assigned a unique number and a cloth label is attached to the bottom right corner of each piece. The labels are made with 100% unbleached cotton and hand sewn with large stitches. The quilt is then surveyed to determine all the factual information about it including the quilt's length and width, how it was made, how the binding was applied, the number of quilting stitches per inch, and what fabrics were used. Any inscriptions are also noted, which are then researched by their genealogy team. Then, the information is entered into their growing database along with any history or genealogical information about the quilt.

Next up, the quilts are actually vacuumed, which may seem odd, but it's an easy way of cleaning quilts gently and removing any dirt that could harm them. The quilts are vacuumed with a soft, flexible screen over them to prevent any damage. They are thoroughly inspected for pests like carpet beetles and moths and afterward they are stored in the museum's state-of-the-art, climate-controlled facility.

Their quilt collection and exhibition spaces are kept at a constant 68° Fahrenheit and 50% humidity to preserve the quilts for many years to come.

Another way their quilts are preserved is by refolding the quilts. As we know, quilts that remain folded in the same fashion for many years often retain permanent creases. To prevent this damage, their quilts are refolded by a team of volunteers every two years. They consciously fold along different lines each time. Most quilts are stored in archival boxes but some are stored flat in drawers or rolled in tubes. While folding, the staff and volunteers wear cotton gloves to keep quilts free from body oils on their hands.

When quilts are brought out for display, they are only displayed for a maximum of one year out of every ten years to minimize light exposure and wear and tear from hanging. Quilts that are on display have 100% cotton sleeves attached to the back of the quilts to help distribute the weight of the quilt evenly. The quilts are thoughtfully hung on the wall so that the center of the quilt falls roughly at a patron's eye level, to give you the very best view.

We can help amazing institutions like the International Quilt Museum keep the thread of history continuing into the future. Help teach new generations the joys of quilting, take them to these museums, and consider donating our own pieces of quilting history for the preservation of the art. Our quilts are not only connections to the past, but also to the future, so make your mark by putting a stitch on the page of history.

**OPEN CAMERA
SCAN CODE
ASK
A QUILT CURATOR!**

Boho Blooms

Bold and beautiful, Boho Blooms brings a
touch of modern simplicity into your home.
This Southwestern-inspired design is easy to
create with straightforward piecing and a bit
of snowballing for an efforlessly chic look.

MATERIALS

QUILT SIZE
75" x 75"

BLOCK SIZE
10" unfinished, 9½" finished

QUILT TOP
1 package of 10" print squares
   - includes pieced border
3¼ yards background fabric
   - includes inner & middle borders

OUTER BORDER
1¼ yards

BINDING
¾ yard

BACKING
4¾ yards - vertical seam(s)
   or 2½ yards of 108" wide

SAMPLE QUILT
Lavender Market by Deborah Edwards
   for Northcott Fabrics

1 cut

Set (6) 10" print squares aside for another project. From each remaining square, cut:

- (1) 4" strip across the width of the fabric.

- (3) 2" strips across the width of the fabric. Set 1 strip from each square aside for the pieced border. Subcut each of the 2 remaining strips into (1) 2" x 4" rectangle and (1) 2" x 6" rectangle. Keep all of the other pieces cut from each square together in a set of (1) 4" x 10" rectangle, (2) 2" x 4" rectangles, and (2) 2" x 6" rectangles.

From the background fabric, cut:

- (7) 6" strips across the width of the fabric. Subcut a **total of (144)** 6" x 2" rectangles.

- (7) 5" strips across the width of the fabric. Subcut a **total of (144)** 5" x 2" rectangles.

- (7) 2" strips across the width of the fabric. Subcut a **total of (144)** 2" squares.

- Set the remainder of the fabric aside for the inner and middle borders.

2 block construction

Mark a line once on the diagonal on the reverse side of each 2" background square. **2A**

Select a set of print pieces. Place a marked square on each corner of the 4" x 10" print rectangle, right sides facing, as shown. **2B**

Sew on the marked lines and then trim the excess fabric ¼" away from the sewn seams. Press and set aside for a moment. **2C 2D**

Place a 5" x 2" background rectangle on each end of a 2" x 6" print rectangle, right sides facing. Mark or crease a diagonal line on each background rectangle as shown. **2E**

Sew on the diagonal lines and then trim the excess fabric ¼" away from the sewn seams. Press. Trim to 2" x 10". **Make 2** and set them aside for a moment. **2F 2G**

Place a 6" x 2" background rectangle on each end of a 2" x 4" print rectangle, right sides facing. Mark or crease a diagonal line on each background rectangle as shown. **2H**

Sew on the diagonal lines and then trim the excess fabric ¼" away from the sewn seams. Press. Trim to 2" x 10". **Make 2**. **2I 2J**

Arrange the 5 units you have created in a row as shown. Sew them together and press. **Make 36**. **2K 2L**

Block Size: 10" unfinished, 9½" finished

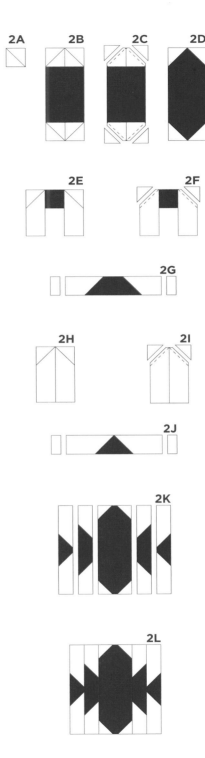

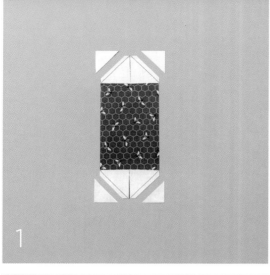

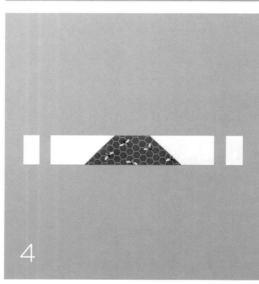

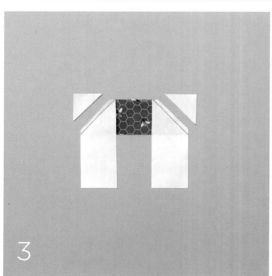

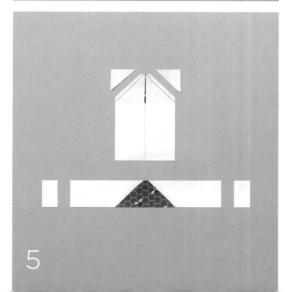

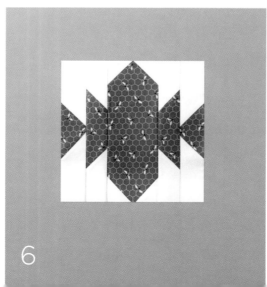

1   Place a marked background square on each corner of a 4" x 10" print rectangle. Sew on the marked line, then trim the excess fabric.

2   Press and set aside for a moment.

3   Place a 5" x 2" background rectangle on each end of a 2" x 6" print rectangle and mark a diagonal line. Sew on the marked lines, then trim the excess fabric.

4   Press, then trim to 2" x 10". Make 2 and set aside for a moment.

5   In a similar fashion, make a unit using (2) 6" x 2" background rectangles and a 2" x 4" print rectangle. Trim the unit to 2" x 10". Make 2.

6   Arrange the 5 units you have created in a row as shown. Sew them together and press. Make 36 blocks.

3 arrange & sew

Refer to diagram **3A** to lay out the blocks in **6 rows of 6**. Notice that every other block is rotated 90°. Sew the blocks together in rows. Press in opposite directions. Nest the seams and sew the rows together. Press.

4 inner border

From the background fabric, cut (12) 1½" strips across the width of the fabric. Sew them together to form a long strip. Cut the inner borders from this strip and then set the remainder of the long strip aside for the middle border. Refer to Borders (pg. 118) in the Construction Basics to measure, cut, and attach the borders. The strip lengths are approximately 57½" for the sides and 59½" for the top and bottom.

5 pieced border

Set (10) 2" x 10" print rectangles aside for another project. Sew the 26 remaining rectangles together to form a long strip. Cut the pieced borders from this strip. Refer to Borders (pg. 118) in the Construction Basics to measure, cut, and attach the borders. The strip lengths are approximately 59½" for the sides and 62½" for the top and bottom.

6 middle border

Pick up the remainder of the long strip you created for the inner border. Cut the middle borders from this strip. Refer to Borders (pg. 118) in the Construction Basics to measure, cut, and attach the borders. The strip lengths are approximately 62½" for the sides and 64½" for the top and bottom.

7 outer border

From the outer border fabric, cut (7) 6" strips across the width of the fabric. Sew them together to form a long strip. Cut the outer borders from this strip. Refer to Borders (pg. 118) in the Construction Basics to measure, cut, and attach the borders. The strip lengths are approximately 64½" for the sides and 75½" for the top and bottom.

8 quilt & bind

Layer the quilt with batting and backing, then quilt. See Construction Basics (pg. 118) to add binding and finish your quilt.

3A

Grandma Mae's Economy Block

Grandmothers the world over know a lot about making do. After all, they've been doing it for years! This economy block quilt is a favorite of theirs because it wastes so little fabric and looks so cute. Put together four sets of these little economy blocks with sashing in between for a design that's definitely granny-approved.

MATERIALS

QUILT SIZE
77¼" x 77¼"

BLOCK SIZE
7¼" unfinished, 6¾" finished

QUILT TOP
1 roll of 2½" print strips
3¼ yards of background fabric

SASHING & INNER BORDER
1½ yards of background fabric

OUTER BORDER
1¼ yards

BINDING
¾ yard

BACKING
2½ yards of 90" wide
    cuddle fabric*

*You can use 4¾ yards 44-45"
wide fabric with vertical seam(s)
or 2½ yards of 108" wide backing
fabric instead.*

SAMPLE QUILT
Graphix Batiks by Island Batik
    and Kona Cotton - Peapod
    by Robert Kaufman

1 cut

Fold each of the 2½" print strips into fourths.

- From 32 strips, cut (2) 2½" squares, (1) 2½" x 3½" rectangle, and (1) 2½" x 1¼" rectangle from each folded strip.
  - Subcut the 2½" x 3½" rectangles in half to yield 1¼" x 3½" rectangles. Keep the (8) 2½" squares and (8) 1¼" x 3½" rectangles from each strip together as a set.

2A

  - Subcut the 2½" x 1¼" rectangles in half to yield a **total of (64)** 1¼" squares and set them aside for the cornerstones.

- From the 8 remaining strips, cut (2) 2½" squares and (1) 2½" x 3½" rectangle from each folded strip. Subcut the 2½" x 3½" rectangles in half to yield 1¼" x 3½" rectangles. Keep these (8) 2½" squares and (8) 1¼" x 3½" rectangles from each strip together as a set. Do not discard the remainder of each strip. After you have completed the cutting, select 4-6 strips that are similar to each other. From the selected strips, cut a set of (4) 2½" squares and (2) 2½" x 3½" rectangles. Subcut the 2½" x 3½" rectangles in half to yield 1¼" x 3½" rectangles.

From the background fabric:
- Cut (3) 1¼" strips across the width of the fabric. Subcut a **total of (81)** 1¼" squares.

- Cut (21) 5" strips across the width of the fabric. Subcut a **total of (162)** 5" squares. Subcut each square in half vertically and horizontally and then along both diagonals to yield a **total of 1,296** setting triangles.

2 sew the setting triangles

Note: You will have 40 pairs of identical blocks and the last block will be created from the set of squares and rectangles you cut from similar fabrics.

Select 32 setting triangles, (2) 1¼" background squares, and a set of print pieces. This will be enough to make 2 identical blocks. Chain piecing makes this project a breeze! If you are comfortable, continue sewing for a few stitches after you've reached the end of the fabric and then slide the next unit under your presser foot without breaking the thread.

Center the long edge of a setting triangle along 1 side of each 2½" print square from your set. Sew along the matched edges. **2A**

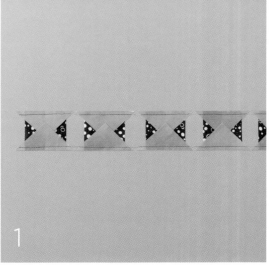

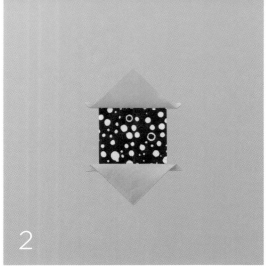

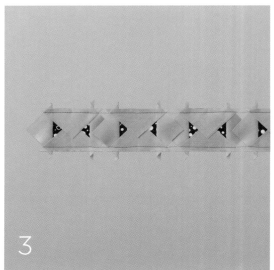

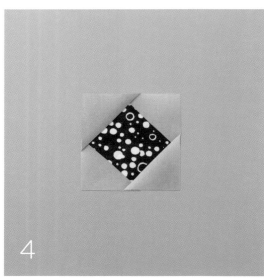

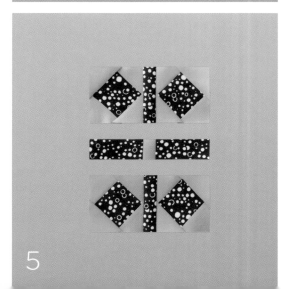

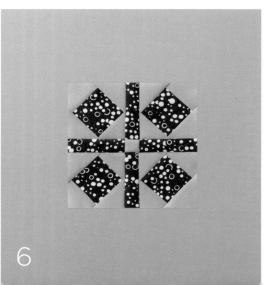

1   Chain piece setting triangles to 2 opposite sides of 8 matching 2½" print squares.

2   Clip the threads between the units, then open and press towards the triangles.

3   Chain piece 2 more setting triangles to the remaining sides of each of the units.

4   Clip the threads between the units, then open and press towards the triangles. Make sure there is ¼" left outside of each point and square each unit to 3½".

5   Sew a 1¼" x 3½" matching print rectangle between 2 of the units to make a row. Press towards the rectangle. Make 2 rows for each block. Sew a 1¼" x 3½" print rectangle to opposite sides of a 1¼" background square. Press towards the rectangles. Lay out the rows as shown.

6   Nest the seams and sew the 3 rows together. Press. Make 81 blocks.

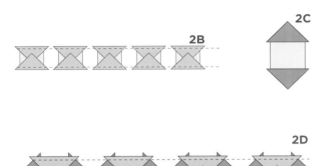

2B

2C

2D

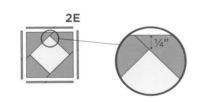

2E

¼"

2F

2G

Clip threads between the units if you like. Place another setting triangle on the opposite side of each square. Sew along the matched edges. Clip the threads between the units and then open and press towards the triangles. **2B 2C**

Repeat to add setting triangles to the remaining sides of each of the print squares in your set. **2D**

Make sure there is ¼" left outside of each point and square each unit to 3½". **2E**

Note: You can make 4 rows in the next step to make 2 identical blocks at the same time.

Sew a 1¼" x 3½" print rectangle between 2 units you just made as shown. Press towards the rectangle. **Make 2** rows for each block. **2F**

Sew a 1¼" background square between (2) 1¼" x 3½" print rectangles. Press towards the rectangles. **Note**: Make a second row if you are making 2 identical blocks. **2G**

Arrange the 3 rows you have created as shown. Nest the seams and sew the rows together. Press. **Make 81** blocks. **2H 2I**

Block Size: 7¼" unfinished, 6¾" finished

3 make sashing

From the background fabric, cut (36) 1¼" strips across the width of the fabric. Set 7 strips aside for the inner border. From the remaining 29 strips, subcut a **total of (144)** 1¼" x 7¼" sashing rectangles.

Select (8) 1¼" print squares and (9) 1¼" x 7¼" sashing rectangles and arrange them in a row as shown. Sew the row together and press towards the sashing rectangles. **Make 8** horizontal sashing strips. **3A**

4 arrange & sew

Refer to diagram **4A** on the next page to lay out the blocks in **9 rows of 9**. Notice how we alternate between light and dark blocks in our quilt. Place a 1¼" x 7¼" sashing rectangle in between each block and sew the rows together. Press towards the sashing rectangles. Place a horizontal sashing strip in between each of the rows. Nest the seams and sew the rows and sashing strips together to form the quilt center. Press.

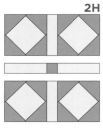

2H

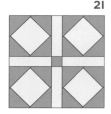

2I

3A

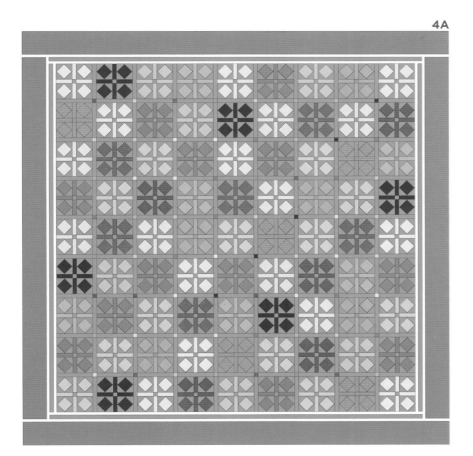

4A

5 inner border

Sew the (7) 1¼" background strips set aside earlier together to form a long strip. Cut the inner borders from this strip. Refer to Borders (pg. 118) in the Construction Basics to measure, cut, and attach the borders. The strip lengths are approximately 67¼" for the sides and 68¾" for the top and bottom.

6 outer border

From the outer border fabric, cut (8) 5" strips across the width of the fabric. Sew them together to form a long strip. Cut the outer borders from this strip. Refer to Borders (pg. 118) in the Construction Basics to measure, cut, and attach the borders. The strip lengths are approximately 68¾" for the sides and 77¾" for the top and bottom.

7 quilt & bind

Layer the quilt with batting and backing, then quilt. See Construction Basics (pg. 118) to add binding and finish your quilt.

Diamond Ring Table Runner

Diamonds set on point are so pretty as is the border for this easy-as-pie table runner. Believe it or not, you don't have to set each diamond on point. It's simplified for you with easy strip piecing! Dress up your table with this Diamond Ring Table Runner and make your next meal sparkle.

MATERIALS

PROJECT SIZE
45" x 17"

SUPPLIES
1 roll of 2½" strips
 - includes pieced border*
½ yard of center rectangle fabric
2 yards of background fabric
 - includes pieced border
½ yard of binding fabric
¾ yard of backing fabric
 - vertical seam

*__Note__: (8) 2½" strips are needed for
this table runner. You may choose to
substitute and cut (1) 2½" strip from each
of 8 different ¼ yard fabrics.*

SAMPLE PROJECT
Cozy Up by Corey Yoder
 for Moda Fabrics

1A

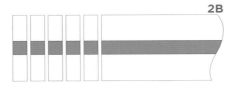

2A

2B

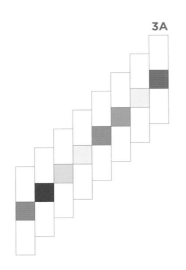

3A

1 cut

From the center rectangle fabric, cut (1) 12" strip across the width of the fabric. Subcut (1) 12" x 40" rectangle.

From the background fabric, cut (17) 4" strips across the width of the fabric. From 1 strip, subcut (4) 4" squares, then cut each square once on the diagonal. **1A**

2 make strip sets

Select (8) 2½" strips of varying colors or prints from your roll of strips. Set the remaining strips aside for another project.

Sew a 4" background fabric strip to both sides of a 2½" strip. Press towards the center. **Make 8**. **2A**

Cut each strip set into 2½" increments. Keep the like colors together. You will need a **total of 40** of these pieced units for your border. The remaining pieces of the strip sets can be used for another project. **2B**

3 make the diamond border

Layout your pieced units in the order you would like them to go around your border. Select the first 8 units and sew them together in an offset fashion as shown. The center squares of each unit should meet at the lower left and upper right corners. Press. This is unit A. **Tip**: Label your units as they are sewn together to keep your color arrangement in order. **3A**

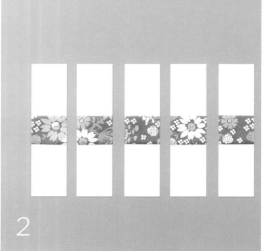

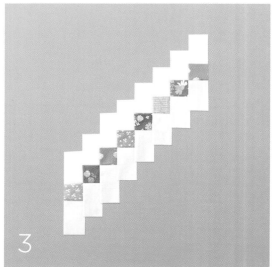

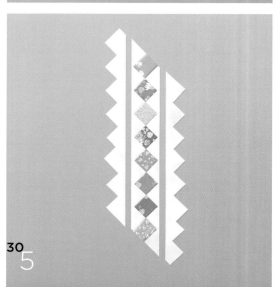

1 Sew a 4″ background fabric strip to both sides of a 2½″ strip. Press towards the center. Make 8.

2 Cut each strip set into 2½″ increments. Keep the like colors together. You will need a total of 40 of these pieced units for your border. The remaining pieces of the strip sets can be used for another project.

3 Sew the first 8 units together in an offset fashion as shown. The center squares of each unit should meet at the lower left and upper right corners. Press.

4 In the same manner, sew the next 4 units together as shown.

5 Lay a unit on your cutting surface as shown. Measure from the center 1¾″ in both directions and trim the unit to 3½″.

6 Repeat for each unit.

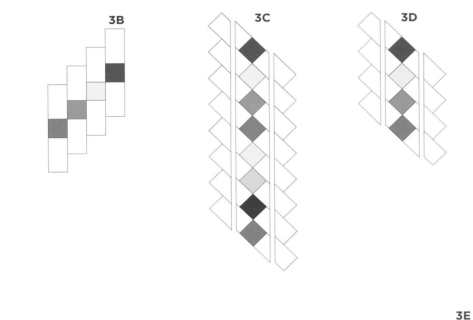

3B

3C

3D

Make a second long unit from the next 8 pieced units in your chosen order. This is unit B.

In the same manner, select the next 4 pieced units from your chosen order and sew them together as shown. This is unit C. **3B**

Continue as before to sew 2 more long units of 8. These will be units D and E. Sew 1 short unit of 4 to be unit F.

Lay a unit on your cutting surface as shown. Measure from the center 1¾" in both directions and trim the unit to 3½". Repeat for each unit. **3C 3D**

3E

Sew units A and B together as shown. Repeat with units D and E. Sew a 4" triangle to either end of both the A/B and D/E borders. **3E**

3F

Sew a 4" triangle to either end of units C and F as shown. **3F**

4 add the borders

Fold the center rectangle in half in both directions and crease to mark the centers along the edges. Also fold each border in half and crease to mark the center.
4A 4B 4C

Lay out your borders around the edges of your center rectangle in the order that you arranged earlier. Match the creases and sew border F to the left side and border C to the right side of your center rectangle. Press towards the rectangle. Trim the ends of the border even with the center rectangle. **4D**

Sew border A/B to the top and border D/E to the bottom. Press towards the center rectangle. Trim the ends of the border even with the sides. **4E 4F**

5 quilt & bind

Layer the table runner with batting and backing, then quilt. See Construction Basics (pg. 118) to add binding and finish your quilt.

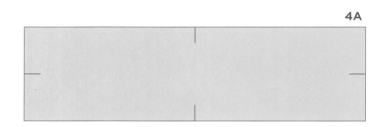

4A

4B

4C

4D

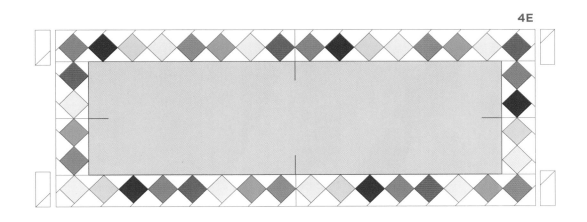

Spools, Stars, & Stitches

Drop everything and stitch up this fabulous Spool Stars and Stitches quilt created with easy strip piecing. It's Jenny's own clever take on a disappearing rail fence quilt. You won't believe how easily these seemingly complex blocks come together. It's absolutely spoolish!

MATERIALS

QUILT SIZE
79" x 79"

BLOCK SIZES
• Spool Block - 8" unfinished, 7½" finished
• "X" Block - 8" unfinished, 7½" finished

QUILT TOP
1 roll 2½" print strips
2½ yards of background fabric
   or 1 roll of 2½" background strips

SASHING & INNER BORDER
1½ yards

OUTER BORDER
1½ yards

BINDING
¾ yard

BACKING
5 yards - vertical seam(s)
   or 2¼ yards of 108" wide

OTHER
Spray starch - recommended

SAMPLE QUILT
Basket of Blooms by Darlene Zimmerman
   for Robert Kaufman

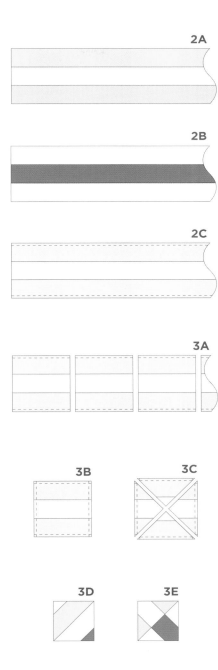

1 cut

From the solid background fabric, cut (33) 2½" strips across the width of the fabric.

2 make strip sets

Tip: Since the strip sets made in this next step will later be cut on the bias, it is helpful to starch them while pressing.

Sew a 2½" print strip to both sides of a 2½" background strip, lengthwise, as shown. Press towards the print. **Make 11**. **2A**

Sew a 2½" background strip to both sides of a 2½" print strip, lengthwise, as shown. Press towards the print. **Make 11**. **2B**

Select 2 strips sets, 1 of each type, and place them right sides together. Sew the strip sets together along both long edges to make a tube. Trim the selvage edges. **Make 11**. **2C**

3 cut block units

Cut each tube into (6) 6½" sections. **3A**

Sew down both open sides of the 6½" tube. **3B**

Cut the sewn units on both diagonals. **3C**

Open and press. Notice that you have 2 different styles of units—spool units will have parallel seam lines and "X" units will have seams that cross 1 another. Starch the units again as needed. **3D 3E**

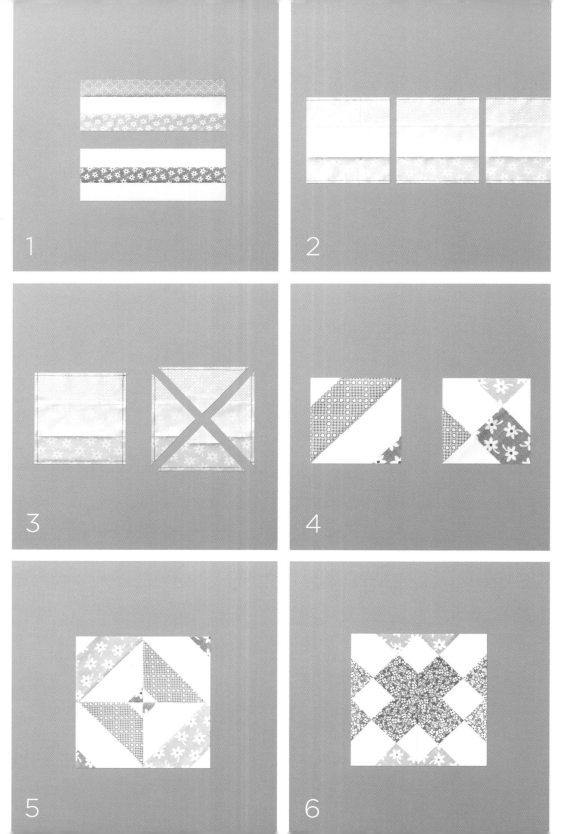

1 Sew a 2½" print strip to both sides of a 2½" solid strip, lengthwise, as shown. Press towards the print. Make 11. Sew a 2½" solid strip to both sides of a 2½" print strip, lengthwise, as shown. Press towards the print. Make 11.

2 Select 1 strip set of each type and place them right sides together. Sew the strip sets together along both long edges to make a tube. Make 11. Cut each tube into (6) 6½" sections.

3 Sew down both open sides of the 6½" tube. Cut the sewn units on both diagonals.

4 Open and press. Notice that you have 2 different styles of units— spool units will have parallel seam lines and "X" units will have seams that cross 1 another. Starch the units again as needed.

5 Select 2 pairs of identical spool units and arrange them in 2 rows of 2 as shown. Sew the units together in rows and press in opposite directions. Nest the seams and sew the rows together. Make 32 spool blocks. Trim to 8" if necessary.

6 Select 2 pairs of identical "X" units and arrange them in 2 rows of 2 as shown. Sew the units together in rows and press in opposite directions. Nest the seams and sew the rows together. Make 32 "X" blocks. Trim to 8" if necessary.

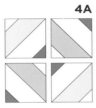

4A

4 spool block construction

Select 2 pairs of identical spool units and arrange them in 2 rows of 2 as shown. Sew the units together in rows and press in opposite directions. Nest the seams and sew the rows together. **Make 32** spool blocks. Set the remaining spool units aside for another project. Trim to 8″ if necessary. **4A 4B**

Block Size: 8″ unfinished, 7½″ finished

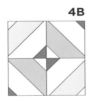

4B

5 "X" block construction

Select 2 pairs of identical "X" units and arrange them in 2 rows of 2 as shown. Notice that the units on each row mirror each other. Sew the units together in rows and press in opposite directions. Nest the seams and sew the rows together. **Make 32** "X" blocks. Set the remaining "X" units aside for another project. Trim to 8″ if necessary. **5A 5B**

Block Size: 8″ unfinished, 7½″ finished

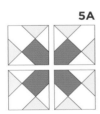

5A

6 make spool stars & large "X" units

Tip: We chose blocks in the same colorway for these units.

Arrange 4 spool blocks into a 4-patch formation as shown to make 1 spool star.

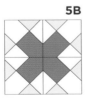

5B

Orient the blocks so the print strip forms a diamond in the center. Sew the blocks into rows and press in opposite directions. Nest the seams and join the rows. Press. **Make 8**. Your spool stars will measure 15½" unfinished. **6A 6B**

Arrange 4 "X" blocks into a 4-patch formation as shown to make 1 large "X" unit. Sew the blocks into rows and press in opposite directions. Nest the seams and join the rows. Press. **Make 8**. Your large "X" units will measure 15½" unfinshed. **6C 6D**

7 arrange & sew

Cut (18) 2½" strips across the width of the sashing and inner border fabric. Subcut (12) 2½" x 15½" vertical sashing strips. Set the remaining strips aside for a moment.

Arrange the spool stars and large "X" units into **4 rows of 4 units** as shown in diagram **7A** on the next page. Add a 2½" x 15½" vertical sashing strip between the units in each row. Sew the rows together and press toward the sashing strips.

Sew the remaining 2½" strips together to make 1 long strip. Trim 5 horizontal sashing rectangles from this strip to the

6A

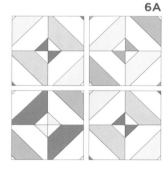

6B

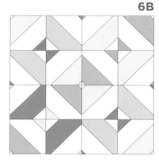

6C

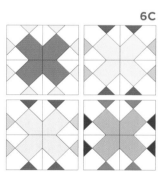

6D

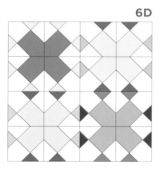

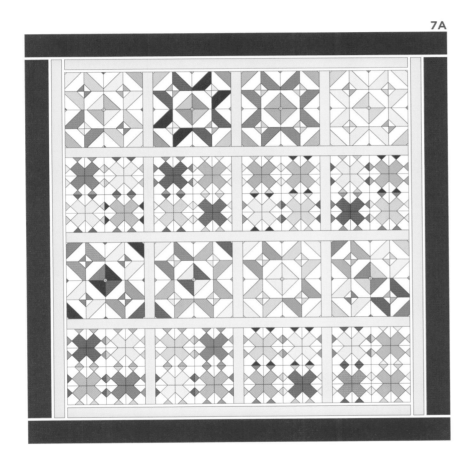

length of your sewn rows—approximately 66½" long. Set the remainder of the long strip aside for the inner border.

Sew the rows together with a horizontal sashing rectangle between each row and on the top and bottom. Press.

8 inner border

Pick up the long 2½" strip you set aside in the last section and trim the side inner borders from this strip. Refer to Borders (pg. 118) in the Construction Basics to measure, cut, and attach the borders. The length is approximately 70½" for the sides.

9 outer border

Cut (8) 5" strips across the width of the outer border fabric. Sew the strips together to make 1 long strip. Trim the borders from this strip. Refer to Borders (pg. 118) in the Construction Basics to measure, cut, and attach the borders. The lengths are approximately 70½" for the sides and 79½" for the top and bottom.

10 quilt & bind

Layer the quilt with batting and backing, then quilt. After the quilting is complete, see Construction Basics (pg. 118) to add binding and finish your quilt.

Minki Kim

Minki Kim is a true artist. She started drawing at age nine and earned a college degree in sculpture. But in all those years of creativity, she had never sewn a stitch. So how did she become one of the world's best-loved fabric and pattern designers? It was a combination of boredom, loneliness, and the irrepressible urge to create.

When Minki married, she and her husband moved from South Korea to the suburbs of Southern California. Soon, a beautiful baby girl—the first of three—joined the family. As a full-time mother, Minki found herself home and alone for hours on end. She often felt isolated, thousands of miles from her dearest friends and family. Her days seemed to run together one after another. She desperately needed a creative outlet.

One day, her husband brought home a sewing machine, but Minki didn't dare touch it. So there it sat, unused, for two years. Finally, Minki gathered her courage. She watched online tutorials to learn a few basic stitching techniques, then constructed a single, no-frills coaster. Bit by bit she gained confidence and skill. (It was another two years before she dared take on zippers...)

As her girls grew, Minki fashioned all sorts of small projects to fit their needs. She made aprons to catch their messes and clever little bags to carry their treasures. And, she began to experiment with a technique she calls sewing illustration, using thread to "draw" scenes depicting the simple magic of everyday life. Those illustrations served as a sort of scrapbook filled with precious memories that might otherwise be forgotten.

OPEN CAMERA
SCAN CODE
WATCH
MINKI KIM'S
BEST TIPS VIDEO

"I wanted to capture the
beauty of ordinary moments...
That is my signature style."
-Minki Kim

"I wanted to capture the beauty of ordinary moments, first with hand embroidery and later with my sewing machine and fabric—literally drawing with thread—to make keepsake snapshots of daily life. That is my signature style."

Eventually, Minki's husband set up a blog and encouraged her to document her projects. She made a habit of posting a single photo every day. Before long, she attracted a sizable following of readers who had fallen in love with Minki's delicate, whimsical style. And that was just the beginning of a successful creative career.

Minki now designs fabric for Riley Blake, including this year's Misty Morning collection. She designs patterns for her own online shop, Sewing Illustrations. She has collaborated with Aurifl to create a block of the month and a curated thread collection. She has published an entire library of fabric and thread project books. And, she still posts regularly on her blog, **minkikim.com**

We are delighted to join forces with Minki for this issue of BLOCK. Speaking of her Misty Morning Drawstring Bag, Minki told us, "We can never have too many drawstring bags; they are so handy and easy to make. But for this project, I wanted to switch things up to create a bag that is truly unique and yet simple enough for all levels of sewists."

Tell us about yourself. What led you to a career in sewing and quilting? Why is your nickname "Zeriano"?
I started sewing as a getaway from being an at-home mom. My husband is a computer programmer and he created my blog. Zeriano is actually his ID. It means "zero + one."

What do you do as a designer for Riley Blake and Aurifil?
I have designed several fabric collections for Riley Blake: Dear Diary, Serendipity, Someday, Moments, Winter's Tale, Hidden Cottage, and Misty Morning.

I was introduced to Aurifil when I wrote my first book, Sew Illustrated, and since then I have been sharing projects that I create with various Aurifil threads. I also curated my own Aurifil collection featuring favorite colors and a range of thread weights, perfect for beginners who would like to try thread drawing.

What led you to designing your own sewing projects and fabric designs?
Sewing projects was my hobby. Designing fabrics was my dream. As a beginner, I was often disappointed with the fabric choices available; they just weren't my style. Now I am lucky to sew with my own fabric lines.

Talk about your style as a designer. How would you describe it?
As a fabric designer, I try to be true to myself and tell my own story: my childhood, favorite days, my small town, day-to-day scenes. My hope is that anyone who sees my designs will know they are by Minki.

Often, your projects are created on a small scale. What do you love about small things?

I enjoy making projects I can finish and enjoy in one day. I especially love to make useful little projects in place of store-bought: lunch bags, fabric baskets, oven mitts, slippers. I do love quilts, but I don't have the patience to make them.

Are you working on any exciting projects?

I just finished a new fabric collection and quilt designs. I am so excited to see what people will create with them!

Where do you find inspiration?

I try to find inspirations around me; a standing mixer cover, fabric bowls for my sewing notions and stationeries on my desk...etc.

What tips do you have for someone who is just starting to sew?

I hope you find the joy of creating something out of the fabric scraps around you. No one can beat someone who really enjoys it.

What's something you've learned recently that has helped you improve your sewing? How do you learn from your mistakes?

I noticed that my finished blocks were always slightly smaller than expected. Finally, I learned about a "scant ¼" seam" by reading an article. I would like to try using "scant ¼" seam" to see how it changes my blocks.

Tell us about something you're proud of that you've made.

I "drew" scenes of my girls playing with their daddy using my sewing machine when they were little. I call this technique "sewing illustration" and in my spare time I still enjoy drawing with threads.

Misty Morning
DRAWSTRING BAG

MATERIALS

PROJECT SIZE
7" wide x 6" high x 6" deep

PROJECT SUPPLIES
(6) 4½" x 10" print fabric
   rectangles for the exterior
1 fat quarter for the lining
(2) 11¾" x 2½" fabric rectangles
   for the casing
(6) 4½" x 10" batting rectangles
(2) 25" lengths of cording

RECOMMENDED
Spray adhesive

OPTIONAL
Embroidery floss

SAMPLE PROJECT
Misty Morning by Minki Kim
   for Riley Blake Designs

1 prep

Use spray adhesive to adhere a 4½" x 10" batting rectangle to the reverse side of each rectangle of exterior fabric.

2 cut

From each of the 6 exterior fabrics/batting rectangles, cut 1 panel piece using the template found at msqc.co/mistymorningbag. **2A**

Use the template to cut 6 lining panel pieces. **2B**

2A

2B

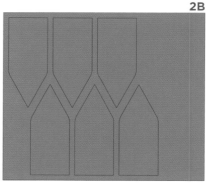

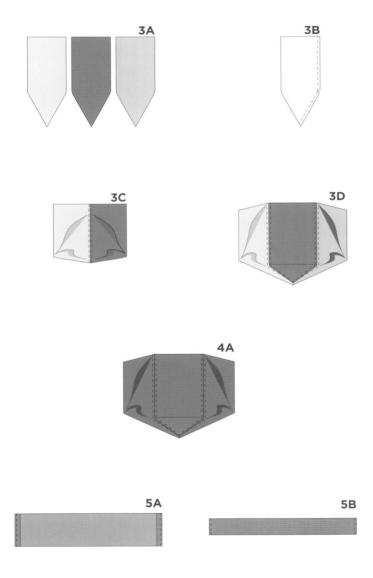

3 assemble the exterior panels

Arrange 3 exterior body pouch pieces in a row as shown. **3A**

Place 2 adjacent panels right sides together and sew along the edge as shown. Clip the corner. **3B**

Open the seam allowance and topstitch ⅛" away on both sides of the seam line. **3C**

Place the third exterior panel on the opposite side of the panel and stitch it to the side of the panel. Open the seam allowance and topstitch as before. **3D** **Make 2**.

4 assemble the lining

Repeat the steps in the previous section using the lining/batting panels to form the 2 lining pieces of the pouch. **4A**

5 make the bag casing

With the wrong sides facing, fold both short edges of a casing strip to the wrong side by ⅜". Press, then fold another ⅜" to enclose the raw edges. Press and stitch along the edges using a ⅛" seam allowance. **5A**

Fold the casing in half lengthwise wrongs sides facing and press again. **Make 2**. **5B**

1

2

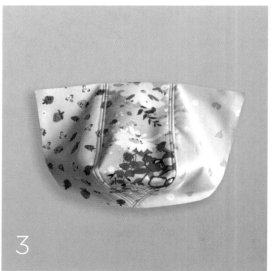

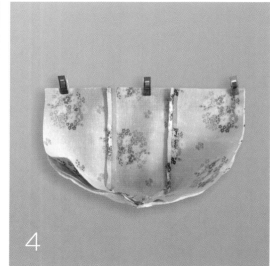

3

4

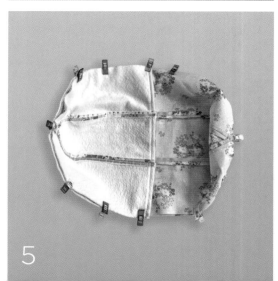

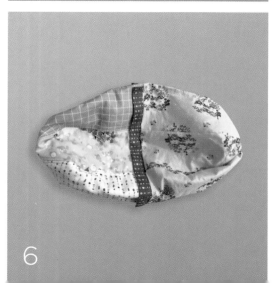

5

6

1 Lay 2 exterior pieces right sides facing. Sew along 1 side. Clip the corner.

2 Open and press. Topstitch on either side of the seam.

3 Add another exterior piece to 1 side, then open, press, and topstitch as before. Make 2 exterior panels. Repeat using the lining pieces to create 2 lining panels.

4 Pin or baste a casing strip to the top edge of 1 exterior panel. Place a lining panel on top of the casing strip and align the edges of the lining panel with the edges of the exterior panel. Sew along the top edge. Make 2.

5 Open and press the 2 bag pieces you just created. Lay the 2 pieces right sides together. Hint: Make sure the lining of the top piece is on top of the lining of the bottom piece. Sew around the perimeter of the pieces leaving a 5" opening along the lining.

6 Turn the bag right side out through the opening. Topstitch ⅛" away from the bottom of the casing. Sew the gap in the lining closed.

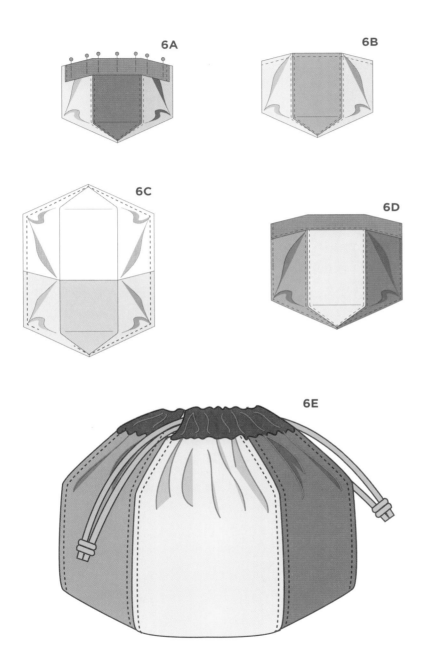

6A

6B

6C

6D

6E

6 assemble the bag

With right sides together, center the casing strip on 1 exterior panel of the pouch, aligning top raw edges. **Tip**: Be sure the ends of your casing strip will not be caught in the ¼″ seam allowance. Pin in place. Baste stitch if you would prefer. Repeat to add the other casing strip to the other exterior panel. **6A**

With right sides together, place a lining panel on an exterior panel and pin in place. Stitch along the top raw edges. Repeat for the other exterior and lining panels. **6B**

With right sides together, place the assembled panels together and stitch all the way around, leaving approximately 5″ open for turning. **6C**

Turn the pouch right side out through the opening and topstitch ⅛″ away from the seam line, making sure not to stitch the lining. **6D**

Handstitch the gap closed. You can machine topstitch if you would prefer.

Thread the cording through the openings at the seams on both ends of the casing.

Optional: Handstitch about ⅛″ away from the casing using 2 strands of embroidery floss.

STACCATO STAR

SEW-ALONG *PART TWO*

QUILT SIZE
97" x 97"

LOVE NOTES STAR BLOCK SIZE
10½" unfinished, 10" finished

MAGIC DIAMONDS BLOCK SIZE
10½" unfinished, 10" finished

ENTIRE QUILT TOP
1-3 packages of Staccato Star
    10" squares*
¼ yard of fabric D**

INNER BORDER
¾ yard**

OUTER BORDER
2 yards**

BINDING
1 yard**

BACKING
8¾ yards - vertical seam(s)
    or 3 yards of 108" wide

OTHER
Missouri Star Drunkard's Path
    Circle Template Set - Small
Clearly Perfect Slotted Trimmer B
    or Bloc Loc 4½" Square Up Ruler

*4 packages of 10" print squares can be substituted for the package of Staccato Star squares. You will need a **total of (148)** 10" squares. Other packages of squares may not have the same number of duplicate prints needed to match the quilt exactly.*

** The ¼ yard of fabric D, ¾ yard for the inner border, 2 yards for the outer border, and 1 yard binding are included in the Staccato Star kit.*

BLOCK SUPPLIES - LOVE NOTES STAR
(2) 10" fabric E squares
(3) 10" fabric F squares
(2) 10" fabric G squares
(3) 10" fabric I squares
(2) 10" fabric J squares
(2) 10" fabric L squares
(3) 10" fabric M squares
(3) 10" fabric N squares

Note: *Fabrics A-D, H, and K are not used in this block.*

OTHER
Clearly Perfect Slotted Trimmer B
    or Bloc Loc 4½" Square Up Ruler

BLOCK SUPPLIES - MAGIC DIAMONDS
(2) 10" fabric J squares
(2) 10" fabric L squares
(2) 10" fabric M squares
(2) 10" fabric N squares

Note: *Fabrics A-I, and K are not used in this block.*

OTHER
Clearly Perfect Slotted Trimmer B
    or Bloc Loc 4½" Square Up Ruler

TOTAL FABRIC REQUIRED IF YOU ARE SELECTING YOUR OWN:
Fabric A - ¾ yard
Fabric B - ¾ yard
Fabric C - ½ yard
Fabric D - ½ yard
Fabric E - 1 yard
Fabric F - 1¾ yards
Fabric G - 1¾ yards
Fabric H - 1 yard
Fabric I - 1 yard
Fabric J - 1 yard
Fabric K - ¾ yard
Fabric L - 2 yards
Fabric M - 1 yard
Fabric N - 1 yard

FABRIC KEY

A E J
B F K
C G L
D H M
I N

PRINT OUT YOUR OWN FABRIC KEY
msqc.co/staccatomakeyourownkey

PRINT OUT PRE-MADE FABRIC KEY
msqc.co/staccatofabrickey

LOVE NOTES STAR
1 cut

Tip: You can save any partial squares you have for increased variety in Part 5.

Gather each of the fabric E, G, J, and L squares, and cut the squares in half vertically and horizontally for a **total of (8)** 5″ squares of each fabric.

From the fabric F, I, M, and N squares:

- From 1 square of each fabric, cut (1) 5″ strip across the width of each square. Subcut a **total of (4)** 5″ squares of each fabric.

- From 2 squares of each fabric, cut (2) 4″ strips across the width of each square. Subcut a **total of (8)** 4″ squares of each fabric.

2 make the half-square triangles

Pair a 5″ fabric E square with a 5″ fabric G square, right sides facing. Sew around the perimeter of the paired squares. Cut through the sewn squares twice on the diagonal. Use the trimmer to square each unit to 3″, then press open—or press, then square to 3″ depending on your trimmer. **Make 32** E/G half-square triangles. **2A**

Repeat using the 5″ fabric F and 5″ fabric I squares to **make 16** F/I half-square triangles. **2B**

Repeat using the 5″ fabric J and 5″ fabric L squares to **make 32** J/L half-square triangles. **2C**

Repeat using the 5″ fabric M and 5″ fabric N squares to **make 16** M/N half-square triangles. **2D**

3 make hourglass units

Mark a diagonal line once on the reverse side of each 4″ fabric I square. Place a marked square atop 4″ fabric F square, right sides facing. Sew on both sides of the marked line using a ¼″ seam allowance. Cut on the marked line. Open and press each towards fabric F. *Do not trim!* **Make 16**. **3A**

Repeat using the 4″ fabric M and 4″ fabric N squares. Press towards fabric N and *do not trim*. **Make 16**. **3B**

Mark a diagonal line, perpendicular to the seam, on the reverse side of each large M/N half-square triangle you just made. **3C**

Lay a marked M/N half-square triangle atop a large F/I half-square triangle, right sides facing with seams nested. Fabrics M and F should be touching, as well as fabrics N and I. Sew on both sides of the marked line as before. Cut on the marked line. **3D**

   2A

   2B

   2C

   2D

   3A

   3B

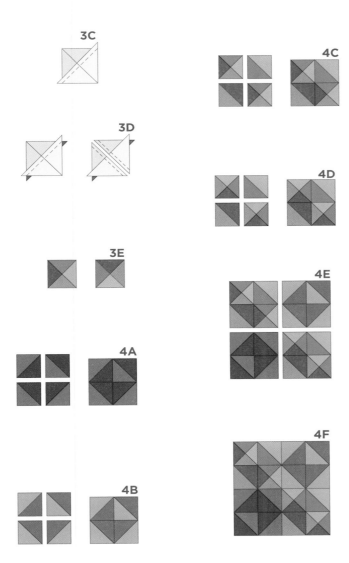

Use the trimmer to square each unit to 3″ then press open—or press, then square to 3″ depending on your trimmer. **Tip**: Line the center seams with the 45° mark of the ruler before trimming. Notice that each set of sewn half-square triangles makes 2 hourglass units with mirrored fabrics. **Make 32** hourglass units. **3E**

4 block construction

Arrange 4 E/G half-square triangles units as shown. Sew the units together in rows. Press the rows in opposite directions. Nest the seams and sew the rows together. Press. **Make 8** E/G quadrants. **4A**

Repeat to sew 4 J/L half-square triangles together as shown. **Make 8** J/L quadrants. **4B**

Arrange 2 hourglass units, 1 F/I half-square triangle, and 1 M/N half-square triangle as shown. Notice that the hourglass units used for this quadrant have the darker fabrics in the top-left. Sew the units together in rows. Press the rows in opposite directions. Nest the seams and sew the rows together. Press. **Make 8** top-left quadrants. **4C**

Again, arrange 2 hourglass units, 1 F/I half-square triangle, and 1 M/N half-square triangle as shown. Notice that the hourglass units used for this quadrant have the darker fabrics in the bottom-right. Repeat to sew the units together to **make 8** bottom-right quadrants. **4D**

Arrange 1 of each style of quadrant as shown. Sew the quadrants together in rows. Press the rows in opposite directions. Nest the seams and sew the rows together. Press. **Make 8** blocks. **4E 4F**

Love Notes Star Block Size: 10½" unfinished, 10" finished

MAGIC DIAMONDS

1 cut

Cut each of the fabric squares for this section in half vertically and horizontally to **make (8)** 5" squares of each.

2 make the half-square triangles

Pair a 5" fabric L square with a 5" fabric M square, right sides facing. Sew a ¼" seam around the perimeter of the paired squares. Cut through the sewn squares twice on the diagonal. Use the trimmer to square each unit to 3", then press open—or press, then square to 3" depending on your trimmer. **Make 32** L/M half-square triangles. **2A**

Repeat using the 5" fabric J and 5" fabric N squares to **make 32** J/N half-square triangles. **2B**

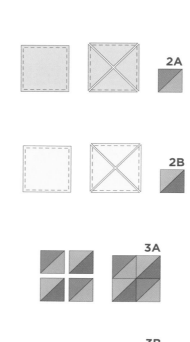

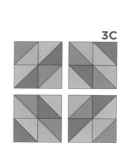

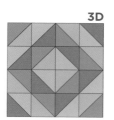

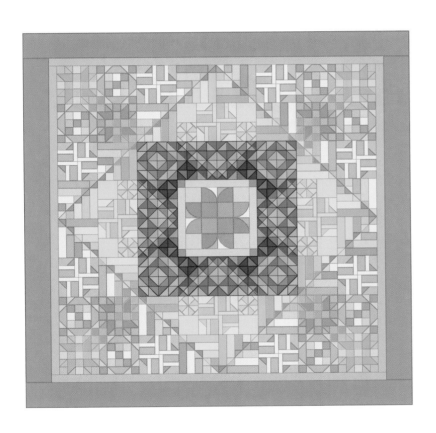

3 block construction

Arrange 2 L/M half-square triangles and 2 J/N half-square triangles as shown. Pay close attention to the direction of the dark and light triangles. Sew the units together in rows. Press the rows in opposite directions. Nest the seams and sew the rows together. Press. **Make 8** A quadrants. **3A**

Again, arrange 2 L/M half-square triangles and 2 J/N half-square triangles as shown. Notice that the dark and light triangles are in opposite directions from the previous units. Repeat to sew the units together to **make 8** B quadrants. **3B**

Arrange 2 A quadrants and 2 B quadrants as shown. Sew the units together in rows. Press the rows in opposite directions. Nest the seams and sew the rows together. Press. **Make 4** blocks. **3C 3D**

Magic Diamonds Block Size: 10½" unfinished, 10" finished

Use Your Strengths To Get Organized

I have written about organization before, but this time I want to talk about the different ways we approach organization and how to use our natural tendencies to our advantages! I'll be the first to admit that my quilting studio is rarely photo-ready, but that's real life. Organization is a way to begin and when we finish a large project or flurry of quilting, it can be a challenge to reset. When you've finished a project, what comes next?

You can tell a lot about a quilter by the state of their sewing space. How we organize can prepare us for our next project and help us feel inspired again or give us the momentum to keep making progress. I am always fascinated by the many different ways people quilt. I have seen beautifully color-coded sewing rooms with shelves arranged just so and not a scrap of fabric out of place. I have seen sewing rooms absolutely filled to the brim with every kind of quilting project imaginable without a single clear surface. Both rooms are brimming with creativity and both have incredible potential.

So, what kind of quilter are you? Here are a few examples to help you hone in on your organizational style and some suggestions to help you find renewed inspiration in your sewing space:

Secret Stasher

If you happen to be a Secret Stasher, you have a sewing room that looks clean... at first glance. But one peek into any of those bins, boxes, or drawers, and a secretly messy stash would be discovered. Secret Stashers really do enjoy organization and you want your sewing room to be clean and functional. It helps you to feel in control when you see open spaces, so you may put something away quickly without thinking too deeply about organization, but that hidden chaos will eventually come to light and cause a feeling of overwhelm. Because Secret Stashers enjoy a streamlined space, you do well with organization that is cleverly hidden, yet easily accessible. Consider a fabric filing system, clear bins with labels, and smaller compartments within drawers. Addressing the mess beneath the surface allows the Secret Stasher to truly relax and enjoy their sewing space.

File It Away

A filing cabinet might become your favorite way to store fabric. Simply fold fabric and drape it over the hanging file. It's compact, fits a lot of fabric, and keeps things neat and organized, yet easily accessible.

Creatively Chaotic

I may or may not identify as a Creatively Chaotic quilter myself. If you're this kind of quilter, you have half-started projects everywhere! The design wall might have a variety of different test blocks, there are piles of fabric everywhere, and everything is out.

List It

A white board with an erasable to-do list is a great addition to your sewing room to help keep track of all the projects you've started. Check them off as you go and see just how creative you can be!

Because Creatively Chaotic quilters like to see everything to know where it is, you do well with visible organization that is easy to maintain. Creatively Chaotic quilters may initially shun the idea that organization is necessary (I plead the fifth on this one), you will discover that organizing according to your visual style will help you to be even more creative. Really! For example, keeping scissors on a visible rack allows you to reach for the pair you have been searching for instead of looking in five different places. Keeping fabric organized by color in open bins allows for fast improvisation without having to search through stacked boxes. Making WIPs visible and accessible keeps you accountable so the projects can be controlled. Allowing the creativity to shine through the chaos is the goal!

Perfectly Imperfect

If you're a Perfectly Imperfect quilter, what you have organized is incredible, but there are many places waiting to be organized that haven't been touched because you don't have the time to do it according to your high expectations. Because you have a tendency toward perfectionism, it would benefit you to allow yourselves to embrace your humanness more fully. Allowing your organization to be "good enough" is a great start. For Perfectly Imperfect quilters, the goal is to solve the problems you see in your sewing space without creating new ones. For example, you don't need to worry about creating the picture-perfect sewing room until you have a workable space. From there, it can be continually improved. If the table is so cluttered that sewing is impossible, clear it off first before creating the cutest display on the shelf. Remember, it's not about perfection, it's about progress!

It's wonderful to have a deep emotional connection to the items you are saving, but don't allow that attachment make you wait for the perfect moment to use your favorite fabrics. The truth is, there is no perfect time. Seize the moment! Use them while you still love them and make something you can truly enjoy.

Make It Work

Start by focusing on the basics of your sewing room. Is your sewing table clear? Is your fabric accessible? Do you have a place to cut and design? Write down a list of the things that aren't working and solve those problems first before trying to perfect what does work. In this case, stick to the old saying, "If it ain't broke, don't fix it!"

Happy Scrapper

If you're a Happy Scrapper, you might have a hard time parting with a single scrap of fabric. You save everything! Happy Scrappers can't turn down free fabric or a good sale and your sewing room is fit to burst! Because Happy Scrappers like to save everything, it might benefit you to deeply analyze the "why" behind your ever-growing stockpile. Once that is addressed, it's easier to take a closer look at your stash without feeling the need to keep something that is no longer serving you.

Donate It

Let your big heart give away things
that no longer serve you to others
who will use them and clear up
some space for yourself.

the STOLEN stitches

PART ONE:
THE SECRECY OF QUILTERS

a fiction novella, in six parts *written by Hillary Doan Sperry*
hillarysperry.com

MISSOURI 1860

Tap, tap, tap.

It was the most timid and irritating knock Abigail had ever heard. She knew it was Lucy on the other side, her carriage had never pulled away. But even knowing they were separated by only a thin slab of painted wood and a door handle, Abigail couldn't bring herself to open the door.

Abigail had never sent Lucy away before. She'd never sent anyone away, but finding out that Lucy had secretly courted her intended, she couldn't let her stay.

Tap, tap, tap.

Abigail's skin crawled with trapped anger.

"Abigail? Please." Lucy's voice was barely more than a whisper of hope on the other side.

Tap, tap, tap.

Maybe Lucy was sorry. Abigail had been so upset when the truth had come out. Maybe they could work things out. Abigail touched the handle. If she didn't open the door, she'd never know. She clicked the latch to the side and swung the door open, certain she looked like an angel of fury as she stared down at her diffident friend.

Lucy looked so forlorn, Abigail softened and almost pulled her back inside to apologize. Until Lucy spoke. "I left my embroideries. We were going to share the dowry linens."

Abigail slammed the door in her friend's face. She could hear the gasp and stormed into the sitting room where they'd been working. The whole table was covered with fabric and thread. She couldn't even look at them. If Lucy had her way the "M" monogrammed on so many of them would be her monogram.

Abigail swept the whole pile up in her arms. She tore through the house flinging the back door open and throwing the lot of them into the air. The pig pen sat across the yard. Grabbing up a handful of the cloths she'd discarded, Abigail marched across the yard, tears streaming down her face.

"I never want to see you again Lucy Fairbanks!" She screamed it loud enough that she hoped her ex-friend would hear her no matter where she stood. "Never again! These linens aren't fit for anyone but the pigs."

The linens sailed over the split rail fence and Abigail's heart lurched. The monogrammed tablecloth caught on the railing not quite making it to the mud below. She stood there staring at it, unable to make herself retrieve the tangled cloth. No matter what Lucy or Abigail did, it was already ruined. Lucy had ruined them all.

A soft sob behind her caught Abigail's attention. She turned to see Lucy frantically gathering the linens blowing through the dirt. Abigail stomped back to the house, past her friend's tear-stained face, with her head held high.

She would not feel bad for what she'd done. Lucy didn't deserve her apology. And Abigail wouldn't give it.

PRESENT DAY

Jenny only froze for a second before she flew into action, pulling loose boards from the rubble and pushing heavier beams out of the way. She couldn't move them far but she pulled back a section of shingles that had torn from the roofing and finally saw the body that was far too still.

Blond curls splayed wildly around the head of a man Jenny didn't recognize. He lay on his back in a puddle of blood. The deep red spreading through the grain of the floorboards. Her breath caught as her throat constricted, trying too late to save herself from breathing in death. She gripped one of the posts, steadying her equilibrium at the sight of a dead man.

The blood formed a perfect circle around his shoulder, clawing its way into the veins of the wood. Several drops accompanied the puddle as if he'd obligingly hung to the side letting it drip two perfect spots before falling to the ground. Tiny cuts scattered across the palms making it look like he'd been digging through a jar of needles.

A splinter dug into Jenny's thumb and she released the broken post. Realizing she'd been holding the side that had torn away. The other half was smooth, like it had been cut. It was cut.

Jenny's heart rate picked up. This wasn't an accident. Someone had wanted the porch to come down.
Aside from his hands, the man had no obvious wounds though the blood made it clear something had happened. Jenny leaned over him, again holding her breath, and trying not to move him. Had he fallen with an accidental injury or had the escaped figure brought the roof down on this man, killing him?

The front door opened and Amanda appeared, her skin glowed under a mask of anger and frustration. Not at all the sweet textiles expert Jenny had met only a few hours before. "What is going on—oh." She pulled back as she realized she was looking at the roof of her porch.

"Amanda?" Jenny didn't know what to say. "There's been an accident."

"What happened?" She asked Jenny, then looked back to the rubble on the porch and took in a sharp breath. "Oh, my gosh. I know him." Amanda lunged forward but couldn't quite reach the man and started climbing over boards and debris.

Jenny tried to stop her. With hands out, she reached for Amanda but she wasn't looking. One of the boards crunched and Jenny's stomach lurched. A loose plank shifted and slid down the side of a broken roof truss, taking Amanda with it. Both women screamed when the board hit the man's shoulder and shoved him off the porch, Amanda stumbled to her knees.

"No. Oh no." the dark-haired woman scrambled back, onto the grass. Blood stained her knees and hands. "Oh, it's Phil. This is him. Is he all right?"

The body hung halfway off the porch caught on the post Jenny had been holding. A ragged cut between his shoulder blades told a bit more of the story, and Jenny had to look away.

With pinched lips Jenny held in her emotions, no longer needing to confirm his death. "He can't be. The roof fell as I pulled up. But he may have already been dead. How did you know him?"

With one hand at her chest and the other hovering over her lips, Amanda gave a halting response. "He worked for us. Helped with repairs on the house." She gestured to the destroyed roof. "Obviously, it needed it. But, Jenny, this is him. I didn't recognize him at the park but Phil was the one taking the embroidery. He was wearing that same burnt orange plaid. And the curly hair … I can't believe he's gone."

Jenny looked at the man again. Phil. There was no obvious pile of white linen bundled beside him. If he'd taken Loretta's tablecloth where was it now and … "What is he doing on your porch?" Amanda didn't answer. Instead, looking over at the neighbor's house, she closed her eyes.

She wasn't doing well but Jenny had so many questions. "Did Phil ever talk to you about Loretta's tablecloth? Why would he want to steal it?"

Amanda raised one trembling hand to her lips then folded her arms across her body. "I don't know. Maybe. I talked about it a lot working up to the guild meeting." Her nostrils flared taking deep breaths, while her hands flitted anxiously from her face to her crossed arms. "Maybe he heard me say how valuable it was." Jenny paused, looking her in the eye. "We need to find you somewhere to sit."

"Umm, there's a bench around the corner." Amanda turned her gaze back to the body.

By the time Jenny got them to the little bench, Amanda's color had gone ashen.

"Where have you been since you left the picnic?" Jenny tried to ask gently.

Amanda looked up, startled. Her fingers paled, gripping the swirls of the metal armrest. "I've been here. I was working on my textile records. I'm tracking a local piece, and Luke's working on the deck, I thought. I haven't seen him since I got home."

"And you didn't hear anything happening on your porch during that time?" It wasn't a very good alibi. In fact, it was hardly one at all.

Amanda shook her head. She was breathing more normally now that she wasn't sitting in front of a dead body. "Not 'till the roof fell off the house. I wear noise-canceling headphones. To be honest, I didn't think anything of it. We've been talking about taking the porch down and expanding it to go the full length of the house. I was just annoyed that Luke hadn't warned me." She swallowed hard and closed her eyes as a breeze blew. "A big southern porch, you know. Good for sipping iced tea and getting to know your neighbors. Now my neighbor is dead."

"Phil was your neighbor?" Jenny took a breath.

"Yeah." Amanda said, "Right over there."

Following Amanda's line of sight Jenny looked at a little brown house facing the wrong way. It had a blue truck in the drive and looked directly at the Jones' home as if the street hadn't always been placed where it was now.

Jenny's phone buzzed in her pocket. She ignored it as Cherry jogged up to the women. Her breathing heavy, worry creased her brow. "I couldn't find them. How long 'till the police arrive?"

"The police?" Amanda squeaked.

"I haven't called. I got distracted." Jenny flinched and patted her hips, pulling out her phone from her back pocket. If she was lucky, it would have service. It didn't. "Do either of you have your phone?"

"I do, but do we have to? No, of course, we do." She wiped her palms against her pants leaving remnants of blood before retrieving her phone. "You're right. I'll just—just a moment." Amanda stood, phone to her ear, and stepped away.

"Is she all right?" Cherry watched the tall woman go. The phone pressed to her ear.

"She's a little upset." Jenny replied. "The body on the porch is her neighbor's."

"Did she kill him?" Cherry hissed, her eyes going wide. "No wait. That was probably the person running away. Was I chasing a killer?"

"I have no idea." Jenny took a breath, unprepared for the question. "I just know the roof fell on him and he worked for Amanda. And she saw him at the park, possibly stealing Loretta's tablecloth."

"I thought she didn't recognize the man at the park?"

"That's what she said, but she knows him now." Jenny glanced at Amanda turning circles in the yard while she talked to the police. "Did you get a look at who was running away?"

"Not really. They were wearing a blue coat. And they went that way. They were gone before I could get after them."

Jenny followed Cherry's line of sight looking back past the Jones' home and across the block. A curtain snapped closed pulling Jenny's attention. An old man had been watching them from the little house on the other side of the yard, under gabled windows capped with gingerbread style trim of blue and pink spindles. The house sat right where the perpetrator would have crossed to the street. Jenny wanted to talk to that man. There were very few fences in Hamilton and he would have had a good view of whoever had gone running from them.

Amanda came back, the phone still at her ear. "Yes. I'm here. No. I won't go anywhere." She held the phone away and covered the speaker. "They want you to stay too."

"Of course." Jenny and Cherry agreed. When Amanda was finally off the phone, Jenny pointed to the house where the old man had been watching. "Do you know all your neighbors?"

Amanda looked at the little house and raised her eyebrows. "Mr. Brown? Sort of. He likes to come outside and yell at my husband. He doesn't like us very well. He'd never hurt anyone though, I don't think. He did threaten Phil once. When Phil was working on the back deck. He said he'd sue us for lowering the property values and told Phil he'd better not do anything else to the house or he'd regret it." She paused her eyes darkening in thought. "But he couldn't have meant this ... could he? He's just an old man." Jenny frowned. "That depends on how angry he was."

"He does carry a pretty heavy cane." Amanda said.

A cane hadn't killed Phil, but maybe it got him in a place where he could be killed.

***

The police documented many of the things Jenny had seen while asking several times for her to tell them what had happened.

Finally, Officer Wilkins clicked his pen closed. "Thank you for your time, ladies. If you don't mind hanging around while we finish up that would be great."

Jenny nodded, and Wilkins crossed the yard talking to Officer Dunn while one of the other officers pulled yellow tape around the porch.
"Now what do we do?" Cherry asked helplessly.

Jenny straightened her shoulders. Helpless wasn't her style. "We wait like they asked," she gave the yard a cursory glance and started walking along the path the fleeing figure had taken. "Over there."

The grassy area between the houses was still wet enough that footprints walked or ran their way through the yard in several areas. Jenny thought she could identify Cherry's footprints, just by their tiny size. There was another pair that looked like tennis shoes but the deepest pair belonged to a pair of boots.

Cherry slid close to Jenny, following her lead all the way to the sidewalk before she stopped them. "You remember they asked us to stay."

"We aren't leaving. We're just looking around." Jenny followed the trajectory a little further past the little Victorian style home. A door slammed and Jenny jumped. An elderly voice yelled into the quiet neighborhood.

"What are you doing here?" He rapped his cane against the porch rail, glaring at them. The man's face was wide and crumpled like it had wilted from his nose to his jowls. She wasn't sure she was ready to meet the cruel Mr. Brown that Amanda had told her about. However, while he was a bit aggressive, unless he had a vintage revolver tucked in the waistband of his caramel-colored suit pants with matching suspenders, his baby blue cane didn't scream killer.

His hair ruffled around a bald patch over the top of his head and, despite a deeply carved frown, his eyes were bright and focused. "What do you want?" he called gruffly, stamping his cane on the porch.

"You wouldn't happen to be Mr. Brown would you?"

He startled as if people didn't usually respond to his demands.

continued on page 110

Easy Tic-Tac-Toe

When you think about it, Tic-Tac-Toe is really a game of hugs and kisses! You'll love this adorably simple quilt featuring nine blocks made up of tiny print squares. It's perfect for playing I Spy with the little ones in your life. Stitch up your blocks, stack them up three in a row, and you'll win every time.

MATERIALS

QUILT SIZE
76" x 76"

BLOCK SIZE
18½" unfinished, 18" finished

QUILT TOP
1 package of 10" print squares

SASHING
¾ yard

INNER BORDER
¾ yard

OUTER BORDER
1¼ yards

BINDING
¾ yard

BACKING
4¾ yards - vertical seam(s)
   or 2½ yards of 108" wide

SAMPLE QUILT
Happy Chance by Laura Heiane for
   Windham Fabrics and Kona Cotton Solids
   - Black & Coal by Robert Kaufman Fabrics

1A

1B

1C

1D

1 make the four-patches

Set (6) 10″ print squares aside for another project.

Lay (2) 10″ print squares together, right sides facing. Sew on 2 opposite sides of the stacked squares. Cut the sewn squares in half parallel to the sewn seams. Open and press. **Make 36**. **1A 1B**

Lay 2 units together, right sides facing with the seams nested. Sew on opposite 2 sides of the stacked squares, perpendicular to the previously sewn seams. Cut the sewn squares in half parallel to the sewn seams. Open and press. **Make 36**. **1C 1D**

2 block construction

Select (4) 4-patches and lay them in 2 rows of 2. Sew the 4-patches together to form rows. Press the seams in opposite directions. **2A**

Nest the seams and sew the rows together. Press. **Make 9**. **2B**

Block Size: 18½″ unfinished, 18″ finished

3 arrange & sew

From the sashing fabric, cut (6) 4″ strips across the width of the fabric. From 3 of the strips, subcut a **total of (6)** 4″ x 18½″ rectangles. Sew the remaining 3 strips together to form 1 long strip. Trim the horizontal sashing strips from this strip.

Refer to diagram **3A** to layout the blocks in **3 rows of 3**. Place a 4″ x 18½″ black rectangle between the blocks and sew the rows together. Press. Measure the length of the rows and cut 2 horizontal sashing strips to this length, approximately 61½″. Sew the rows together with the horizontal sashing strips between. Press.

4 inner border

From the inner border fabric, cut (7) 2½″ strips across the width of the fabric. Sew the strips together to make 1 long strip. Trim the borders from this strip. Refer to Borders (pg. 118) in the Construction Basics to measure, cut, and attach the borders. The lengths are approximately 61½″ for the sides and 65½″ for the top and bottom.

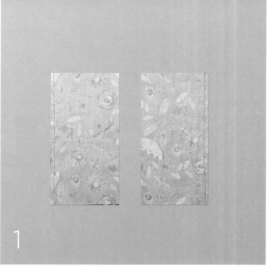

1

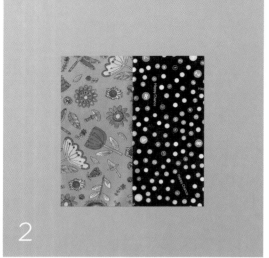

2

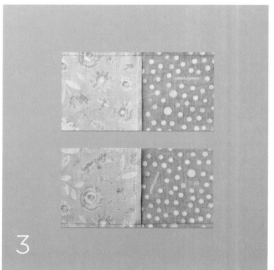

3

4

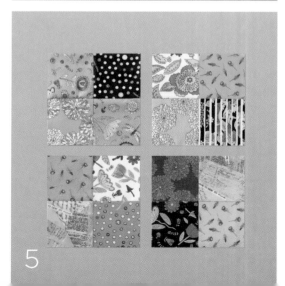

5

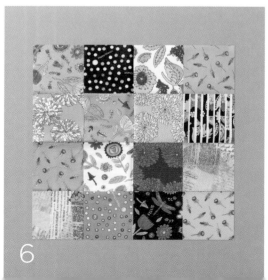

6

1 Place (2) 10″ print squares right sides together. Sew on 2 opposite sides of the stacked squares. Cut the sewn squares in half parallel to the sewn seams.

2 Open and press towards the darker fabric. Make 36 units.

3 Lay 2 units with different print fabrics right sides together with the seams nested. Sew on 2 opposite sides of the stacked squares, perpendicular to the previously sewn seams. Cut the sewn squares in half parallel to the seams you just sewed.

4 Open and press. Make (36) 4-patches.

5 Arrange (4) 4-patches in 2 rows of 2.

6 Sew the 4-patches together to form rows and press the seams in opposite directions. Nest the seams and sew the rows together. Make 9 blocks.

2A

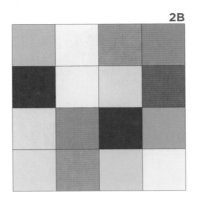

2B

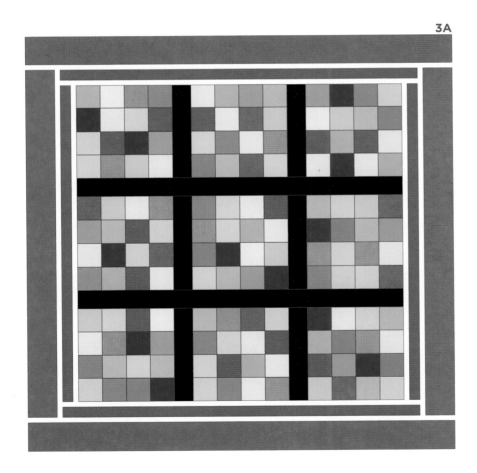

3A

5 outer border

From the outer border fabric, cut (7) 6″ strips across the width of the fabric. Sew the strips together to make 1 long strip. Trim the borders from this strip. Refer to Borders (pg. 118) in the Construction Basics to measure, cut, and attach the borders. The lengths are approximately 65½″ for the sides and 76½″ for the top and bottom.

6 quilt & bind

Layer the quilt with batting and backing, then quilt. After the quilting is complete, see Construction Basics (pg. 118) to add binding and finish your quilt.

REMEMBER ME

THE HISTORY OF SIGNATURE QUILTS

A signature tells a story all by itself—the loops, the slant, the size, and the character of the lettering all bear the personality of the individual who signed it. And signature quilts tell wonderful stories too. Also known as album, autograph, freedom, and friendship quilts, signature quilts have a beloved history that dates back centuries. They are a visual representation of relationships and contain stories that capture a moment in time.

The local Missouri Quilt Museum had the honor of hosting a lovely display of signature quilts that features eight quilts from all over Missouri, each one telling its very own story. Signature quilts were initially created for many reasons including honoring well-respected individuals in the community, sending off friends who were moving far away as a token of remembrance, commemorating engagements, celebrating marriages, marking coming of age ceremonies, and even helping to raise funds for important causes.

In this signature quilt exhibit, each quilt was created for a special purpose and each has a unique legacy. The most recent quilt in the exhibit was created during the famous "Friday Nite Sew" sessions here in town and it features a signature block sewn by Natalie and Jenny. The oldest quilt in this collection dates all the way back to 1898. It's from a church group in Southern Missouri, who often gathered together for quilting bees. One of the quilts held most dear in this collection originates from the heart of Quilt Town, U.S.A. Sewn in the 1940s, it contains the names of families that lived in Hamilton for many generations. A couple of the other signature quilts showcase perfectly imperfect children's artwork. How sweet! But the most popular quilt in this exhibit— popular for obvious reasons—is the Celebrity Signature quilt.

Celebrity Signature Quilt

Made in 1974 to help raise funds for the Palos Verdes Junior Women's Club in California, an organization that supports women and children in crisis, the Celebrity Signature quilt showcases over 50 famous signatures. This incredible piece of history is signed by the likes of Dick Van Dyke, Burt Reynolds, Barbara Streisand, Bob Hope, Ed McMahon, Carol Burnett, Sammy Davis Jr., Sonny and Cher, Princess Margaret, John Wayne, Richard Nixon, Dean Martin, Frank Sinatra, Mary Tyler Moore, Ronald Reagan, and many others. Each of these celebrities were given a white cotton square of fabric and asked to sign it. The maker then carefully embroidered each name with great attention to detail and then the signature squares were pieced together into a remarkable quilt. What a treasure!

It's intriguing to wonder about the lives of those who signed these quilts and the experiences of the quilters themselves. Dakota Redford said, "I love signature quilts! The stories that they tell resonate deeply in my heart! Why were these people together? What were their relationships with one another? What was the mark they made on history? Searching out the personal histories of the makers of quilts is one of my favorite jobs in curating!" We may not know the answers to all of these questions, but we can get a glimpse into the lives of these quilters when we see the amazing creations they've left behind.

For this issue, Jenny created a modern version of this historical quilt style. It is signed by members of the Doan family and will surely be treasured for generations. Each block has a center square with a diagonal strip of white sashing that's the perfect size for a signature. Collect the signatures of your loved ones and stitch up your own keepsake. It's a great gift for special events like marriages, anniversaries, graduation, birthdays, holidays, and more and makes memories that will last a lifetime or longer. Learn how to make your own signature quilt Jenny-style on page 98.

How to Sign a Signature Quilt

Here are a few tips to make sure your signature quilt lasts for a long time. When you are signing fabric, it's important to make sure you are using high quality fabric markers that won't bleed or fade. Missouri Star Fabric Markers, made by the renown Japanese brand Marvy Uchida, are fine tip, water-resistant fabric markers that are perfect for lettering on fabric— and the ink absolutely stays put! There's no need to steam or iron, simply write and wash. This fabric marker is nontoxic and has a fine bullet-shaped point that stays sharp.

But it's also important to know what type of fabric to use. The fabric we recommend for signature quilt blocks is called "PFD," which means "prepared for dye." PFD fabric is unbleached and no optic whiteners are added, which gives you a great canvas for fabric markers. The ink will absorb into the fabric permanently for signatures that will stick around.

How to Embroider Your Signatures

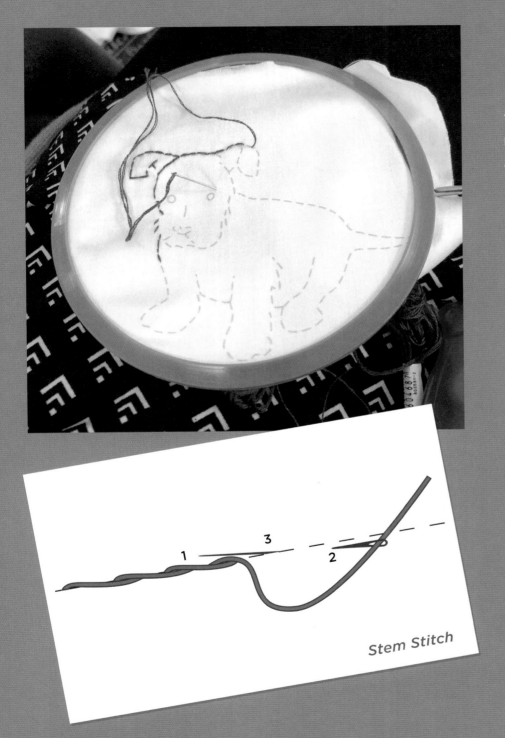

Stem Stitch

You don't have to embroider your signature blocks, but if you would like to, here's an easy stitch to try. It's called a "stem stitch" and it works great for signatures. A stem stitch is a smoother stitch that's a bit different from a backstitch in that you don't just stitch back to the end of the last stitch, you actually go further and stitch halfway back alongside the previous stitch, creating a ropelike stitch that's a bit thicker.

Here's how you do it:

- -

1. Take your first complete stitch about ¼" of an inch long and pull your thread back up through the fabric, but don't pull your thread completely taut just yet.

2. Put your needle back down into the fabric halfway between the beginning and the end of your first stitch.

3. Pull your first stitch taut and then come back up through the fabric ¼" in front of your last stitch.

4. Work back into your last stitch as you had done previously.

- -

And there you have it! A perfect little stem stitch for your signature quilts.

INMATES CREATE
quilts for kids

"The Restorative Justice Program gives offenders the chance to grow and give back to their community by making beautiful quilts for foster children."

In Missouri alone, there are nearly 20,000 children enrolled in the state's foster care system. According to the Missouri Department of Social Services Children's Division, nearly every region in Missouri has seen a double-digit increase in the number of children admitted into the system since 2010. You don't have to know a lot about foster care or have been involved in the system yourself to know it's not the ideal situation for any child. The average age of a foster child is 8 years old, children older than 9 years are 50% less likely to be adopted, and a considerable number of kids age out of the system without a loving home or legal guardian.

For so many children, growing up in foster care is often confusing, frustrating, and even scary. Sometimes they don't know how long they have with their current foster family, when their potential adoptive parents will get that final stamp of approval, and if they'll be spending their 18th birthday alone. It goes without saying that these children need comfort and kindness, and many foster kids are receiving it from the most unlikely of places: a prison in Licking, Missouri.

At the South Central Correctional Center in Licking, Missouri, there is a group of inmates who spend their days in front of sewing machines, providing comfort and love to those in need one stitch at a time. These inmates are part of the Restorative Justice Program, a program devoted to giving offenders the chance to grow and give back to their community, like making beautiful quilts for foster kids. The inmates who participate in the quilting program not only get to personally choose their child, they get to do the designing, gridding, and quilting. The sizing of these quilts is based on the age range of the kids, so ages 0-3 would receive a baby size quilt, 4-12 receive a twin size quilt, and 13-18+ receive a queen size quilt.

Many children in foster care don't have much in terms of personal items or belongings because of how often they move from home to home, so when they receive a care package containing a colorful quilt personalized with their name, a handmade hat, school supplies, and/or toiletries, it reminds them they have not been forgotten. For inmate Rod Harney, that's exactly what it's all about. "You see the names of these kids in foster care; you see a 1-year-old or 2-year-old, and it kind of breaks your heart. But that lets us know we're human still. You can't express enough how it feels to do it," said Harney.

And it's not just the children who benefit from this program, the men making these precious quilts receive something in return, too. Being surrounded by the hum of sewing machines in a room full of color provides these men with a temporary escape from their day-to-day prison life, and allows them to engage with their community again. It just goes to show that making a quilt is as much a gift as receiving one.

If you would like to donate to the program, the inmates are always in most need of:
fabric | batting | thread | yarn

Ready to donate?
Contact Marty Meyer, the Restorative Justice Coordinator, at **marty.meyer@doc.mo.gov**.

For more information about the Restorative Justice Program at South Central Correctional Center, you can contact Joe Satterfield at **Joseph.Satterfield@doc.mo.gov**.

Red and White Antique Lace

This year I'm making red and white quilts together with my sewing buddy, Cherry. Red and white quilts became our focus after I saw a gorgeous display of these classic quilts. I absolutely fell in love with the idea of making them all year long! There's no shortage of incredible red and white quilts and I don't think I'll ever tire of this lovely color combination.

The first red and white quilt I made is a version of Antique Lace, one of my favorite traditional quilt patterns. Keep an eye on my Instagram to see even more of these pretty two-color quilts pop up all year long.

Jenny's Crumb Quilt

Every morning I like to do a little something for myself before I settle in to the day's work. It helps me jumpstart my creativity! I keep a large bin behind my desk where I save all my leftover bits and pieces of fabric. Because I am a make-do girl, I love being able to make a quilt with fabric I already have. I grab a large handful of these scraps and sew them together until I get approximately a 10" piece and then I trim my crumb block down to a nice 10" square. I save up enough of these crumb blocks until I can create an entire quilt. And then I start all over again! In this case, I also added a complimentary piano key border with low volume fabrics. Learn how to make your own eclectic crumb quilt in our January Triple Play tutorial. It's a lot of fun and it's incredibly easy.

Daydreaming Wings

MATERIALS

DAYDREAMING WINGS SIZE
18¼" x 17"

PROJECT SUPPLIES
¾ yard of main fabric
¼ yard of accent fabric
½ yard of Heat n Bond Lite
¾ yard of Peltex Single Sided
Fusible Stabilizer
¾ yard of fusible fleece - 20" wide
1 yard of ½" elastic

WING TEMPLATES
msqc.co/daydreamingwingstemp

Note: You can find an appliqué set for the Daydreaming Wings, Monarch butterfly wings, and templates for dragon wings at **msqc.co/daydreamingwingstemp** The supply list and instructions for the Monarch Wings and Dragon Wings can be found in our digital version of BLOCK.

1 make the wings

Print and cut out the wing and appliqué templates for your chosen wings at the link above. Follow the instructions on the wing templates to assemble the single wing template.

- From the main fabric, cut (1) 18½" strip across the width.
  - Subcut (2) 18½" x 20" rectangles.

- From the accent fabric, cut (1) 8" strip across the width.
  - Subcut (1) 8" x 17½" rectangle.

- From the Heat n Bond Lite, cut (1) 7½" strip across the width.

- From the Peltex, cut (1) 18½" strip across the width.
  - Subcut (1) 18½" x 20½" rectangle.

- From the fusible fleece, cut (1) 18½" strip across the width.
  - Subcut (1) 18½" x 20½" rectangle.

1A

template edge on fold

1B

2A

2B

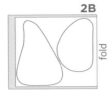

fold

2C

2D

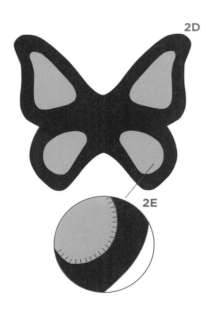

2E

Follow the manufacturer's instructions to adhere the wrong side of the fabric to the glue side of the Peltex. Repeat to adhere the fusible fleece to the reverse side of the second fabric rectangle.

Fold the Peltex in half, right sides of the fabric facing. Line up the straight edge of the template with the fold and trace 1 wing shape onto Peltex. **1A**

Cut out on the traced line. **1B**

Repeat to fold, trace, and cut 1 wing shape from fusible fleece/fabric rectangle.

2 add appliqué

Trace the accent shapes onto the paper side of the 7½" strip of Heat n Bond Lite, close to the left edge. **2A**

Follow the manufacturer's instructions to adhere the full Heat n Bond strip to the reverse side of the 8" x 17½" accent rectangle. Fold the fused rectangle in half, right sides of fabric facing. Keeping the rectangle folded, cut out the accent shapes. You will have mirrored versions of each shape. **2B 2C**

Adhere the accent shapes onto the fusible fleece-backed wings following the diagram. **2D**

Use a straight, zigzag, or decorative stitch around the accent pieces. **2E**

3 add the straps

Cut (2) 14″ lengths of elastic. Clip the end of 1 piece of elastic to the top of the fusible-fleece backed wing and the other end to the bottom of the wing, spaced ¾″ to 1″ from the center. Repeat for the second elastic piece. There should be about 1½″ to 2″ between the elastic ends. Stitch over the elastic ends several times within the ¼″ seam allowance. Pin the extra elastic to the center of the wings to keep it out of the way. **3A**

With right sides together, lay the Peltex-backed wing on top of the fusible-fleeced backed wing. Pin or clip in place. Stitch around the outside of the entire wings using a ¼″ to ½″ seam allowance, leaving a 4″ opening along 1 straight edge. Clip into the seam allowance around the curves, being careful not clip through any stitches. **3B**

Turn the wings right sides out through the 4″ opening. Poke out the edges with fingers or the eraser end of a pencil. Remove the pins holding the elastic and move the elastic to the back of the wings. Topstitch ⅛″ from the edge around the perimeter, closing the hole. **3C**

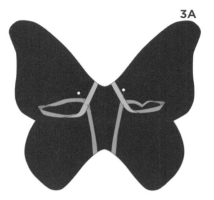

3A

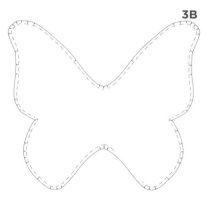

3B

3C

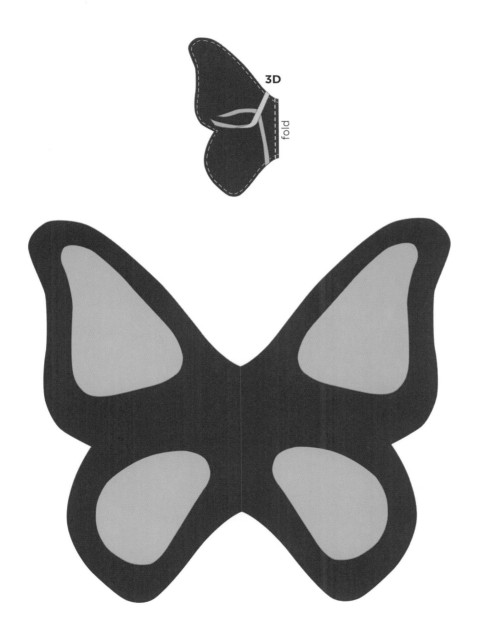

3D

fold

Optional: If your sewing machine can handle the bulk, fold the wings together with the appliqué facing in and stitch a straight vertical line along the center about ½" away from centerfold. **3D**

**OPEN CAMERA
SCAN CODE
WATCH
TUTORIAL TO MAKE
DAYDREAMING WINGS**

Periwinkle Plates

Patchwork periwinkle stars in two sizes are appliqued onto this quilt in the same style as Dresden plates, hence the name! Give machine applique a try, we think you'll enjoy it even more than you imagine. These lovely Periwinkle Plates are as pretty as a picture.

MATERIALS

QUILT SIZE
78½" x 78½"

BLOCK SIZE
14" unfinished, 13½" finished

QUILT TOP
1 package of 10" print squares
1 package of 5" print squares
3¾ yards of background fabric

BORDER
2½ yards

BINDING
¾ yard

BACKING
5 yards - vertical seam(s)
   or 2½ yards of 108" wide

OTHER
Missouri Star Small Periwinkle
   (Wacky Web) Template for
   5" Charm Packs - optional
Missouri Star Mini Periwinkle
   (Wacky Web) Template for
   2.5" Squares - optional
10½ yards of (20" wide)
   lightweight fusible interfacing

SAMPLE QUILT
Mint Crush by Lisa Audit for Wilmington
   Prints, Cotton Supreme Solids
   - Twilight by RJR Fabrics

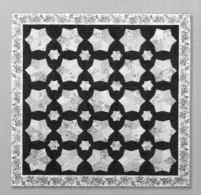

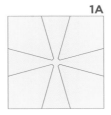

1A

1B

2A

2B

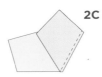

2C

2D

1 cut

Note: You can set aside (4) 10″ print squares and (18) 5″ print squares for another project if you wish. You can also cut extra periwinkles as described below for added variety and set aside any leftover periwinkles after sewing the quilt top.

From each 10″ print square, cut 4 small periwinkle pieces as shown. **1A**

From each 5″ print square, cut 4 mini periwinkle pieces as shown. **1B**

From the background fabric, cut (9) 14″ strips across the width of the fabric. Subcut the strips into a **total of (25)** 14″ squares.

From the fusible web, cut (25) 15″ strips across the width of the interfacing.

2 make the large periwinkles

Lay 2 small periwinkle pieces of contrasting fabrics right sides facing and sew along 1 long edge. Open and press to 1 side. **2A 2B**

Lay another small periwinkle piece on top of the unit, right sides facing. Sew along 1 long edge. Open and press to 1 side. **Make 2** halves. **2C 2D**

Lay the 2 halves right sides facing. Sew together along the longest edge. Open and press. **Make 25** and set them aside for now. Set any remaining small periwinkle pieces aside for another project. **2E**

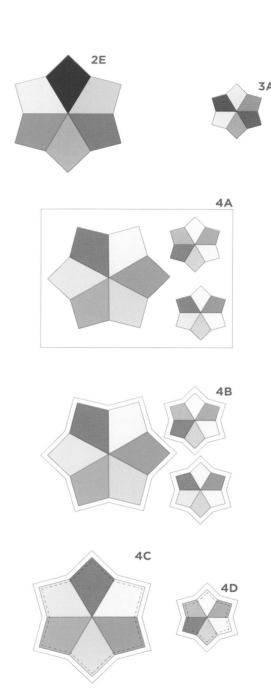

3 make the small periwinkles

Repeat the steps in the previous section to **make 16** mini periwinkles using the mini periwinkle pieces. Set any remaining mini periwinkle pieces aside for another project. **3A**

4 add the interfacing

Place the periwinkles, on top of the interfacing strips as shown. The adhesive side of the fusible interfacing should be against the right side of the periwinkles. Pin in place.

Note: 17 of the strips will only have the small periwinkle pinned to them. **4A**

Roughly cut the interfacing around each periwinkle to separate. **4B**

Sew along the perimeter of each periwinkle with a ¼″ seam allowance. **4C 4D**

4E

4F

Trim the excess fabric from the outside points and cut a slit into the inside corners, making sure not to cut into the seam. Carefully cut a slit in the interfacing and turn the periwinkle plate right side out. Gently poke out the corners of the periwinkle plate. Do not press. **4E 4F**

5 block construction

Fold each 14″ background square in half in both directions. Finger press to mark the centers. **5A**

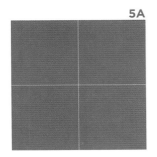

5A

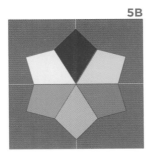

5B

Lay a small periwinkle atop a background square with the center seam aligned to 1 fold and the points of the top and bottom aligned with the other. Follow the manufacturer's instructions to fuse the periwinkle to the background fabric. **5B**

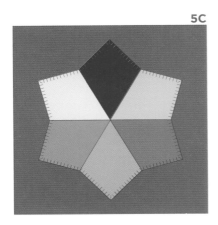

5C

Appliqué around the perimeter of the periwinkle using a blanket or small zigzag stitch. **Make 25**. **5C**

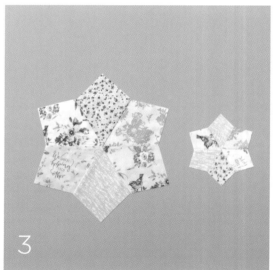

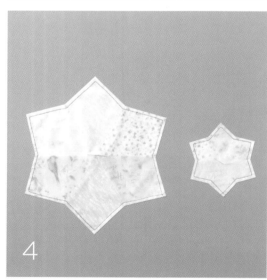

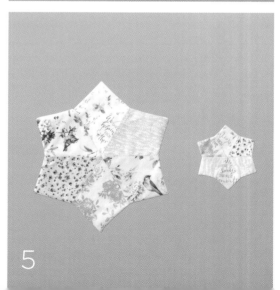

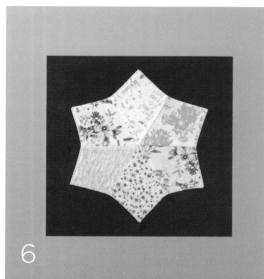

1 Lay 2 small periwinkles right sides facing and sew along 1 long edge. Open and press to 1 side.

2 Lay another small periwinkle on top of the unit with right sides facing. Sew along 1 long edge, then open and press to 1 side. Make 2 halves like this using different fabrics.

3 Sew the 2 halves together. Open and press. Make 25 large periwinkles. Follow the same steps using the mini periwinkle pieces to create 16 small periwinkles.

4 Place the periwinkles face down on the interfacing, pin in place and roughly cut around the edge. Sew along the perimeter using a ¼" seam allowance. Trim the excess fabric from the outside points and cut a slit into the inside corners, making sure not to cut into the seam. Carefully cut a slit in the interfacing.

5 Turn the periwinkle right side out and gently poke out the corners. Do not press!

6 Fold each 14" background square in half in both directions. Finger press to mark the centers. Place a large periwinkle on top aligned with the folds. Press in place, then appliqué around the edge using the stitch of your choice.

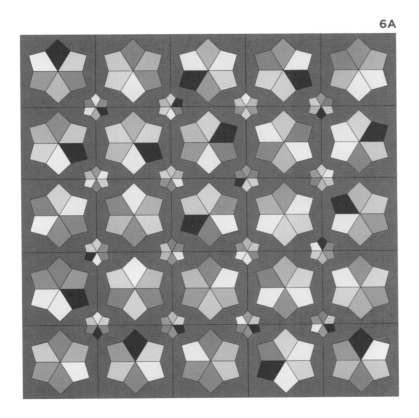

6A

Block Size: 14″ unfinished, 13½″ finished

6 arrange & sew

Refer to the diagram **6A** to arrange the blocks in **5 rows of 5**. Pay close attention to the orientation of the blocks.

Note: The mini periwinkles will get sewn on in the next step. Sew the blocks together in rows. Press in opposite directions. Nest the seams and sew the rows together. Press. **6A**

Lay the mini periwinkles atop the quilt top as shown. Use the seams connecting the blocks together as a guide for placing the periwinkles. Follow the manufacturer's instructions to fuse the periwinkles to the quilt top.

As you did before, appliqué around the perimeter of the periwinkles using a blanket or small zigzag stitch.

7 border

From the outer border fabric, cut (4) 5½″ strips along the *length of the fabric*. Cut all of the strips so that the same motifs are centered within each border strip cut. This will likely create a strip of unused fabric between each border strip you cut. Set these smaller strips aside for another project.

Cut the borders from the (4) 5½″ strips. Your quilt top should measure approximately 68″ square at this point. If your quilt top measures more than this, add on the difference to the strips you cut. The strip lengths are approximately 83″ for each side.

Mark the center of each side of the quilt top with a pin. Mark the center of each border strip in the same manner. Be sure the side you mark on your border strips is the side you will sew to the quilt top.

Measure 34″, or half of the size of your quilt top, in both directions on each border strip and mark these points with pins. **Note**: The distance between these 2 pins should be the same length and width as your quilt top.

Match the centerpoint of 1 border strip to the centerpoint of 1 side of your quilt top, then pin together at the center. Match the edges of the quilt top to the outer pinned points on the border strip. Pin the border to the quilt. Mark ¼″ in from each edge of the quilt top with a removable ink pen.

Sew the border strip to the quilt top starting and stopping at the mark placed ¼″ from each end. Backstitch at each end. Press towards the border. Repeat to attach all 4 borders. **7A**

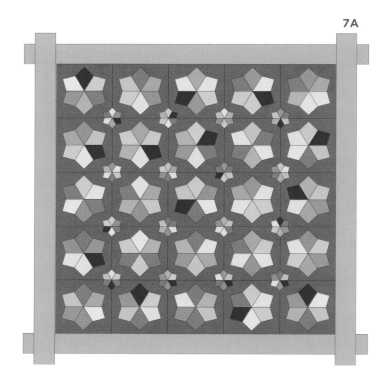

7A

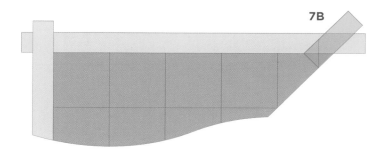

7B

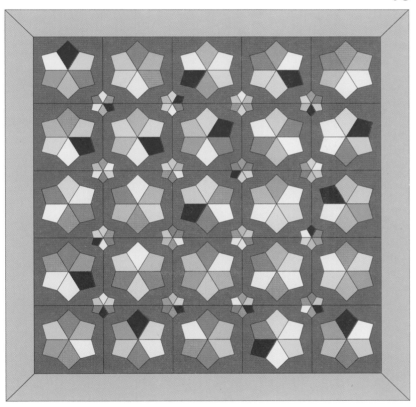

7C

Fold the quilt on the diagonal, right sides facing, and line up 2 adjacent border strips. Pin the tails of the border strips together to prevent them from shifting. Use an acrylic ruler with a 45° line to mark the mitered edge of the border as shown. **7B**

Begin at the inside corner where the seams of the border meet and sew on the marked line. Backstitch at the beginning and end of your seam. Open to check that it lays correctly and there are no puckers. Refold and trim the excess border fabric ¼" away from the seam. Repeat for the remaining 3 corners. **7C**

8 quilt & bind

Layer the quilt with batting and backing, then quilt. See Construction Basics (pg. 118) to add binding and finish your quilt.

Signature Quilt

Making signature quilts is a beloved tradition that dates back to the 1800s. Preserve treasured memories with this project featuring handwritten signatures from dear friends and family captured on quilt blocks. You'll create a piece of history that will last a lifetime, or longer!

MATERIALS

QUILT SIZE
73" x 73"

BLOCK SIZE
8½" unfinished, 8" finished

QUILT TOP
1 roll of 2½" print strips
1 yard of print fabric for center squares*
¼ yard of print fabric for cornerstones*
3½ yards of background fabric
  - includes sashing and inner border

OUTER BORDER
1¼ yards

BINDING
¾ yard

BACKING
4½ yards - vertical seam(s)
  or 2¼ yards of 108" wide print fabric*

OTHER
Missouri Star Marker

*__Note__: We chose to use a print backing
fabric for our center squares, cornerstones,
and quilt backing. If you chose the same, you
will only need 5½ yards or 2¼ yards of 108"
wide print backing.

SAMPLE QUILT
Bee Plaids by Lori Holt
  for Riley Blake Designs

2A

2B

2C

2D

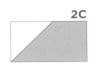

2E

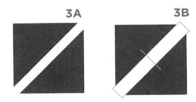

3A   **3B**

3C

1 cut

Note: Keep all squares and rectangles organized in sets of 4 matching like-sized pieces.

From the roll of 2½" print strips, cut:
- 24 strips into (8) 2½" x 4½" rectangles.

- 12 strips into (16) 2½" squares.

- 1 strip into (4) 2½" x 4½" rectangles and (4) 2½" squares. Add these to the pieces previously cut. You will have a **total of 49** sets of 4 matching 2½" x 4½" rectangles and a **total of 49** sets of 4 matching 2½" squares.

- Set the remainder of the strips aside for another project.

From the print fabric for the center squares, cut (6) 4½" strips across the width of the fabric. Subcut a **total of (49)** 4½" center squares from the strips.*

From the print fabric for the cornerstones, cut (2) 1½" strips across the width of the fabric. Subcut a **total of (36)** 1½" cornerstones from the strips.*

*__Note__: If you are using 108" wide backing for the center squares and cornerstones, cut:
- (3) 4½" strips along the **length** of the fabric. Subcut (18) 4½" squares from 2 strips and (13) 4½" squares from the third strip for a **total of (49)** 4½" squares.

- Cut the remainder of the third strip into (3) 1½" strips. Subcut a **total of (36)** 1½" cornerstones from these strips.

From the background fabric, cut:
- (25) 2½" strips across the width of the fabric. Subcut a **total of (392)** 2½" squares.

- (35) 1½" strips across the width of the fabric.
  ◦ Subcut 25 strips into (3) 1½" x 8½" rectangles and (2) 1½" x 7" rectangles. You will need a **total of (49)** 1½" x 7" rectangles. Set the extra rectangle aside for another project.

  ◦ Subcut 2 strips into (4) 1½" x 8½" rectangles each.

  ◦ Subcut 1 strip into (1) 1½" x 8½" rectangle. You will have a **total of (84)** sashing rectangles.

  ◦ Set 7 strips aside for the inner border.

2 flying geese units

Mark a diagonal line once on the reverse side of each 2½" background square. **2A**

Select a set of (4) 2½" x 4½" print rectangles. Place a marked square on the left end of each print rectangle as shown. Sew on the marked line, then trim the excess fabric ¼" away from the sewn seam. Press. **2B 2C**

Place another marked square on the right end of each unit as shown. Sew, trim, and press as before. **Make 49** sets of 4 matching flying geese units. **2D 2E**

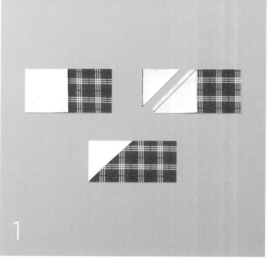

1

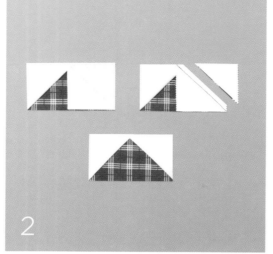

2

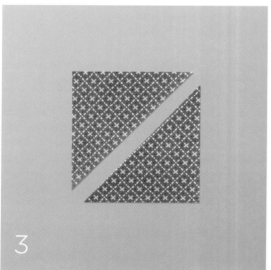

3

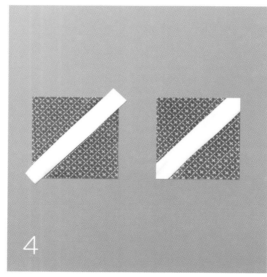

4

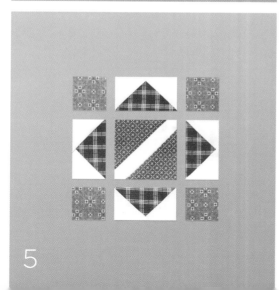

5

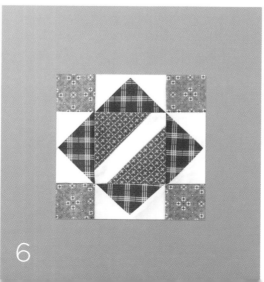

6

1 Place a marked square on the left end of a print rectangle as shown. Sew on the marked line and then trim the excess fabric ¼" away from the sewn seam. Press.

2 Place another marked square on the right end of each unit as shown. Sew, trim, and press as before. Make 49 sets of 4 matching flying geese units.

3 Cut a 4½" backing square in half diagonally.

4 Fold the long edge of each triangle and a 1½" x 7" background rectangle in half and press a crease. Sew the triangles to both sides of the rectangle as shown. Press. Trim to 4½". Make 49.

5 Arrange 1 set of 2½" print squares, 1 set of flying geese, and 1 center square in 3 rows of 3 as shown.

6 Sew the units together in rows and press towards the squares. Sew the rows together. Press. Make 49.

3 make center units

Cut a 4½" backing square in half diagonally. **3A**

Fold the long edge of each triangle and a 1½" x 7" background rectangle in half and finger press a crease. Align the creases and sew the triangles to both sides of the rectangle as shown. Press. **3B**

Trim the unit to 4½". **Make 49. 3C**

Note: Use a permanent marker to sign the background strip in each center unit.

4 block construction

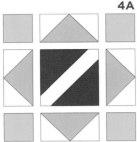

4A

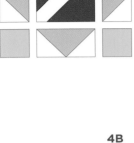

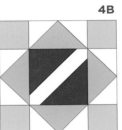

4B

Arrange 1 set of 2½" print squares, 1 set of flying geese, and 1 center square in 3 rows of 3 as shown. The prints in the sets should differ. Sew the units together in rows and press towards the squares. Nest the seams and sew the rows together. Press. **Make 49. 4A 4B**

Block Size: 8½" unfinished, 8" finished

5 horizontal sashing

Arrange 7 sashing rectangles and 6 cornerstones in a row as shown. Sew the units together and press towards the rectangles. **Make 6. 5A**

6 arrange & sew

Arrange the blocks into **7 rows of 7 blocks** as shown in diagram **6A**. Sew the blocks together with sashing rectangles in between each block to form the rows. Press towards the sashing rectangles. Sew the rows together with a horizontal sashing strip in between each row. Press.

7 inner border

Sew the (7) 1½" background strips together to make 1 long strip. Trim the borders from this strip. Refer to Borders (pg. 118) in the Construction Basics to measure, cut, and attach the borders. The strip lengths are approximately 62½" for the sides and 64½" for the top and bottom.

5A

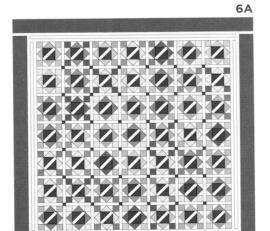

6A

8 outer border

Cut (7) 5" strips across the width of the outer border fabric. Sew the strips together to make 1 long strip. Trim the borders from this strip. Refer to Borders (pg. 118) in the Construction Basics to measure, cut, and attach the borders. The lengths are approximately 64½" for the sides and 73½" for the top and bottom.

9 quilt & bind

Layer the quilt with batting and backing, then quilt. After the quilting is complete, see Construction Basics (pg. 118) to add binding and finish your quilt.

Stars & Stripes Table Runner

Oh my stars and stripes! Featuring two bright eight-pointed stars with a row of rainbow stripes in between, this brilliant table runner will light up your home from breakfast to dinner. Pull it out for a special occasion or use it every day to make the ordinary extraordinary!

MATERIALS

PROJECT SIZE
52" x 15"

BLOCK SIZE
11½" unfinished, 11" finished

PROJECT TOP
1 package of 2½" solid strips
¼ yard of background fabric

BORDER
½ yard

BINDING
½ yard

BACKING
1 yard - vertical seam(s)

SAMPLE PROJECT
Kona Cotton - Bright Rainbow Palette
   by Robert Kaufman Fabrics

1A

fold | 2½" x 6" | 2½" x 4" | fold

1B

2½" x 11½" | fold

1C

4" | 4" | 4" | 4" | 4" | 4" | 4" | 4"
2½" 2½" 2½" 2½" 2½" 2½" 2½" 2½" 2½" 2½" 2½" 2½" 2½" 2½" 2½" 2½"

2A

2B

2C

1 cut

From your package of 2½" strips:

- Select 2 matching solid strips. Fold the strips in half and then in half again. From the folded strips cut a 6" rectangle and a 4" rectangle. You will get 4 rectangles from each cut. You need a **total of (8)** 2½" x 6" solid rectangles and a **total of (8)** 2½" x 4" solid rectangles. **1A**

- Select (7) 2½" solid strips. Fold the strips in half and cut (1) 11½" rectangle. You will get 2 rectangles from each cut and need a **total of (13)** 2½" x 11½" solid rectangles. **1B**

- Set the remaining strips aside for another project.

From the background fabric:

- Cut (1) 4" strip across the width of the fabric.
  - Subcut (8) 4" squares. **1C**

- Cut (1) 2½" strip across the width of the fabric.
  - Subcut (16) 2½" squares. **1C**

Set the remaining fabric aside for another project.

2 make the star blocks

Each block is made from (4) 2½" x 4" solid rectangles, (4) 2½" x 6" solid rectangles, (4) 4" background squares, and (8) 2½" background squares.

Mark a diagonal line once on the reverse side of each 2½" background square. **2A**

Place a marked background square on 1 end of a 2½" x 4" solid rectangle with right sides facing, as shown. Sew on the marked line. Trim ¼" from the sewn line and press open. **Make 4** short units. **2B**

Place a marked background square on 1 end of a 2½" x 6" solid rectangle with right sides facing, as shown. Sew on the marked line. Trim ¼" from the sewn line and press open. **Make 4** long units. **2C**

Sew a short unit to the right side of a 4" background square. Press towards the short unit. Sew a long unit to the bottom. Press towards the long unit. **Make 4** quadrants. **2D 2E**

Arrange 4 quadrants as shown. Sew the quadrants together in rows and press in opposite directions. Nest the seams and sew the rows together. Press. **Make 2** blocks. **2F 2G**

Block Size: 11½" unfinished, 11" finished

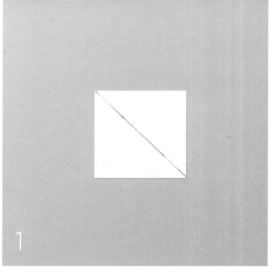

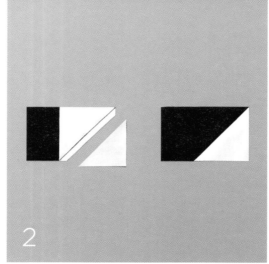

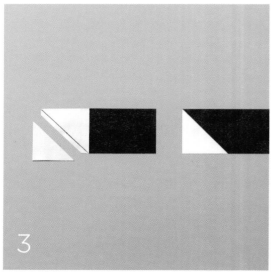

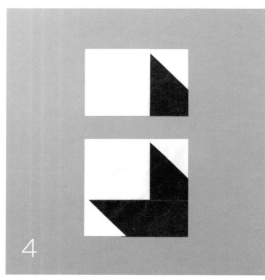

1 Mark a diagonal line once on the reverse side of each 2½" background square.

2 Place a marked background square on 1 end of a 2½" x 4" solid rectangle with right sides facing as shown. Sew on the marked line. Trim ¼" from the sewn line and press open. Make 4 short units.

3 Place a marked background square on 1 end of a 2½" x 6" solid rectangle with right sides facing as shown. Sew on the marked line. Trim ¼" from the sewn line and press open. Make 4 long units.

4 Sew a short unit to the right side of a 4" background square. Press towards the short unit. Sew a long unit to the bottom. Press. Make 4 quadrants.

5 Arrange 4 quadrants as shown. Sew the quadrants together in rows. Press in opposite directions.

6 Nest the seams and sew the rows together. Press. Make 2 blocks.

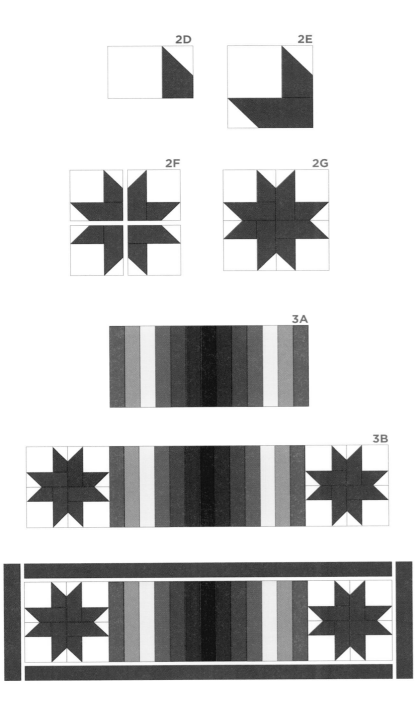

3 assemble & sew

Sew the (13) 2½" x 11½" solid strips together lengthwise as shown. **Note**: After sewing each strip press towards the darker fabric. **3A**

Sew a star block to either side of your strip set. Press. **3B**

4 border

Cut (3) 2½" strips across the width of the border fabric. Refer to Borders (pg. 118) in the Construction Basics to measure, cut, and attach the borders. The strip lengths are approximately 48½" for the top and bottom and 15½" for the sides. Notice that the longer borders are sewn on first, then the short ends.

5 quilt & bind

Layer the project with batting and backing, then quilt. See Construction Basics (pg. 118) to add binding and finish your project.

Jenny was pleased to see him smile as she climbed the porch steps.

It didn't last. He recovered his scowl and looked around. "Been George Brown since the day I was born. What do you want? Are you from the VA? Wait." His frown deepened. With narrowed eyes, he held up his cane like a sword. "Did you bring cookies?"

Jenny hesitated, trying to connect the dots in his questions and failing. "No. My name is Jenny, and this is Cherry. I don't have cookies, but Cherry makes really good snickerdoodles if you'd like some."

"Why would I want 'em? I'm diabetic. Are you trying to kill me?" His voice was cranky, but he didn't leave. Just thumped his way across the porch of the well-kept home. "People are always bringing cookies."

Jenny's mouth twitched up at the corner. She wasn't supposed to like this guy. "Okay, I promise I won't bring you any cookies, but I'd love to ask a few questions."

George settled onto a chair with both hands on the cap of his cane and rested his chin on the back of his hands. "What do you want to know?"

"One of your neighbors just died. Someone—"

"Who?" He asked cutting her off, and Jenny's smile twitched again.

She needed to keep herself under control. They were talking about murder. "Phil. I don't know his last name."

"Bruno," George announced.

Jenny was going to ask about the person who'd run away past his home, but at the name Bruno, she stopped. "Phil Bruno? Do you know his wife's name?"

George grumbled something and stamped his cane against the porch again. "I can't remember. Kara, Keely? Something with a K."

"Kelly," Jenny said the name, a pit forming in her stomach.

"That's it!" Mr. Brown's eyes lit up and his wrinkles rolled together into lifted brows, and he shot a victorious smile at Jenny. "Kelly. You got it."

A queasy feeling rolled through her and without looking at either Cherry or George, she accepted the confirmation. "I know her."

"From the Guild?" Cherry grabbed Jenny's elbow, the shock still resonating through her.

When Jenny didn't say anything else Cherry took over. "Mr. Brown, George, we got here shortly after Mr. Bruno was killed and we were just wondering if you saw anyone run past your house? Maybe twenty minutes ago?"

George's brow furrowed, and he settled his chin back onto his cane. "No. There was a lot of yellin' back of my wife's house this morning. Phil was back and forth but recently? Just you two snoopin' around."

"Your wife's house? She doesn't live here?" Cherry asked.

George frowned. "She was my wife. Are you stupid? We lived here before she died. Judy passed away several years back. I met her when she lived in that beauty, there." He pointed his cane at the Jones' house. "Met her, courted her, kissed her. We lived next door our whole lives. Now people are coming in changin' things and ruinin' the neighborhood."

"How do you mean?" Jenny settled herself on the porch steps anxious to know.

"They called 'em improvements," George scoffed. "They added a monstrosity of a room out the back and they were fixin' to expand the porch."

"But the main house didn't change, did it?" Cherry's voice was ripe with confusion.

"Well, no. But the porch. Judy and I shared our entire courtship on that porch. There was a secret compartment in one of the posts, you know. We would exchange love notes there. And they were going to destroy it. New posts, new rails ... new everything. So, I tore it down." He laughed like it was a big joke, not taking into account the fact that a body had been found beneath his work.

George opened his mouth and paused. "You're not going to go and tattle on me, are ya? Telling the police I tore down that porch?"

I saw them over there. They were takin' it down anyway. Did them a favor."

Jenny shot an anxious glance at Cherry. "You said you heard yelling ... any idea who that was?"

George's eyes lit up again. "Mr. Jones. He had Phil by the shoulder and threw him out of the house. He was yelling at him about his wife and keepin' away from her. Phil's not been much of a straight shooter. But if Luke was throwin' him out that means no more work on my Judy's house. I'm not sure what happened after that. See, that's when I was lookin' for the saw. Mr. Jones had gone, and I knew it was my chance to get things ready. I got the saw and cut right through the post and my Judy's secret cubby. Nobody's using that hiding place but me and her." This time when he settled back in his chair his wide face had formed into a smug grin.

Jenny cleared her throat and leaned forward. "You didn't see what happened there a little bit ago, did you?"

"You mean who killed Phil. No. I've been napping." George got up and walked inside, leaving his cane behind.

Cherry shot Jenny a glance, "Does that mean he's done?" Jenny didn't respond. He'd left the door open and just inside the door sat a pair of boots. The feet were coated in a dark stain, the soles a thick muddy brown.

"How badly do you think he needs his cane if he just leaves it behind?" Jenny asked tiptoeing across the porch.

Cherry shrugged as Jenny picked up the cane and looked it over for signs of mud.

"I don't know. Why?" Cherry asked.

Footsteps sounded and Jenny set the cane back in its place and hurried back to the steps as George reappeared, a protein bar in his hand.

Her mind was racing. "George," Jenny asked, "when was the last time you were over at the Jones' house. I'm sure it's easy to walk over and check on things."

George chuckled and stretched his legs out. "I don't go over there. It's not good for my heart."

"But you cut through the porch this morning, didn't you?"
"Did I? I can't remember." He winked, like she was now in on his joke.

Jenny forced a breathy laugh. Cherry gave her a look that said she was considering looking up phone numbers for the looney bin. Jenny glanced back at George's cane; she couldn't help it. She hadn't found mud on it but red streaks caked into the rubber stopper. Red. Blood red. The word echoed in her mind as Cherry thanked him for his time.

Jenny was already on her way down the steps. Her phone buzzed again but she didn't answer, just tried to move faster.

Cherry grumbled and did a little skip step to keep up as Jenny headed down the sidewalk. "What's the hurry?"

"George is lying. Did you see the muddy boots in the house? They match the prints we were following. And his cane. Cherry, there was blood on his cane."

"That's impossible. I couldn't have been chasing George. The figure didn't have a cane. Besides, I may not be an Olympian, but I'm pretty sure I could have caught an old man, even with a head start."

Jenny's heart rate had picked up and as she crossed into the grass her breathing was heavy. "Then George wasn't the one running away, but he was there. And I don't think it was yesterday or this morning."

Her phone buzzed again and Jenny yanked it from her pocket. "What is it?" She hissed at the device.

She'd missed several calls and a text, from Loretta of all people. Jenny. Call me. Now. They're all gone.

to be continued...

111

Boho Blooms

QUILT SIZE
75" x 75"

BLOCK SIZE
10" unfinished, 9½" finished

QUILT TOP
1 package of 10" print squares
  - includes pieced border
3¼ yards background fabric
  - includes inner & middle borders

OUTER BORDER
1¼ yards

BINDING
¾ yard

BACKING
4¾ yards - vertical seam(s)
  or 2½ yards of 108" wide

SAMPLE QUILT
Lavender Market by Deborah
  Edwards for Northcott Fabrics

QUILTING PATTERN
Paisley Feathers

PATTERN
14

Grandma Mae's Economy Block

QUILT SIZE
77¼" x 77¼"

BLOCK SIZE
7¼" unfinished, 6¾" finished

QUILT TOP
1 roll of 2½" print strips
3¼ yards of background fabric

SASHING & INNER BORDER
1½ yards of background fabric

OUTER BORDER
1¼ yards

BINDING
¾ yard

BACKING
2½ yards of 90" wide
   cuddle fabric*

*You can use 4¾ yards 44-45"
wide fabric with vertical seam(s)
or 2½ yards of 108" wide
backing fabric instead.

SAMPLE QUILT
Graphix Batiks by Island Batik
   and Kona Cotton - Peapod
   by Robert Kaufman

QUILTING PATTERN
Jacobean

PATTERN
18

Diamond Ring Table Runner

PROJECT SIZE
45" x 17"

SUPPLIES
1 roll of 2½" strips
   - includes pieced border*
½ yard of center rectangle fabric
2 yards of background fabric
   - includes pieced border
½ yard of binding fabric
¾ yard of backing fabric
   - vertical seam

***Note**: (8) 2½" strips are needed
for this table runner. You may
choose to substitute and cut
(1) 2½" strip from each of 8
different ¼ yard fabrics.

SAMPLE PROJECT
Cozy Up by Corey Yoder
   for Moda Fabrics

QUILTING PATTERN
Posies

PATTERN
26

Spools, Stars, & Stitches

QUILT SIZE
79" x 79"

BLOCK SIZES
- Spool Block - 8" unfinished, 7½" finished
- "X" Block - 8" unfinished, 7½" finished

QUILT TOP
1 roll 2½" print strips
2½ yards of background fabric or 1 roll of 2½" background strips

SASHING & INNER BORDER
1½ yards

OUTER BORDER
1½ yards

BINDING
¾ yard

BACKING
5 yards - vertical seam(s) or 2¼ yards of 108" wide

OTHER
Spray starch - recommended

SAMPLE QUILT
Basket of Blooms by Darlene Zimmerman for Robert Kaufman

QUILTING PATTERN
Spools of Thread

PATTERN
34

Misty Morning Drawstring Bag

PROJECT SIZE
7" wide x 6" high x 6" deep

PROJECT SUPPLIES
(6) 4½" x 10" print fabric rectangles for the exterior
1 fat quarter for the lining
(2) 11¾" x 2½" fabric rectangles for the casing
(6) 4½" x 10" batting rectangles
(2) 25" lengths of cording

RECOMMENDED
Spray adhesive

OPTIONAL
Embroidery floss

SAMPLE PROJECT
Misty Morning by Minki Kim for Riley Blake Designs

PATTERN
46

TEMPLATE
msqc.co/mistymorningbag

Staccato Star Sew Along
Part 2

PRINT OUT PRE-MADE FABRIC KEY
msqc.co/staccatofabrickey

PRINT OUT YOUR OWN FABRIC KEY
msqc.co/staccatomakeyourownkey

BLOCK SUPPLIES - LOVE NOTES STAR
(2) 10" fabric E squares
(3) 10" fabric F squares
(2) 10" fabric G squares
(3) 10" fabric I squares
(2) 10" fabric J squares
(2) 10" fabric L squares
(3) 10" fabric M squares
(3) 10" fabric N squares

Note: *Fabrics A-D, H, and K are not used in this block.*

OTHER
Clearly Perfect Slotted Trimmer B or Bloc Loc 4½" Square Up Ruler

BLOCK SUPPLIES - MAGIC DIAMONDS
(2) 10" fabric J squares
(2) 10" fabric L squares
(2) 10" fabric M squares
(2) 10" fabric N squares

Note: *Fabrics A-I, and K are not used in this block.*

OTHER
• Clearly Perfect Slotted Trimmer B or Bloc Loc 4½" Square Up Ruler

TOTAL FABRIC REQUIRED IF YOU ARE SELECTING YOUR OWN:
Fabric A - ¾ yard
Fabric B - ¾ yard
Fabric C - ½ yard
Fabric D - ½ yard
Fabric E - 1 yard
Fabric F - 1¾ yards
Fabric G - 1¾ yards
Fabric H - 1 yard
Fabric I - 1 yard
Fabric J - 1 yard
Fabric K - ¾ yard
Fabric L - 2 yards
Fabric M - 1 yard
Fabric N - 1 yard

PATTERN
50

Easy Tic-Tac-Toe

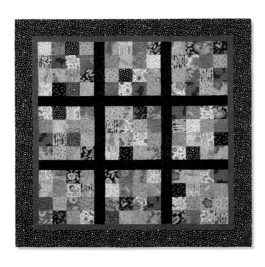

QUILT SIZE
76" x 76"

BLOCK SIZE
18½" unfinished, 18" finished

QUILT TOP
1 package of 10" print squares

SASHING
¾ yard

INNER BORDER
¾ yard

OUTER BORDER
1¼ yards

BINDING
¾ yard

BACKING
4¾ yards - vertical seam(s) or 2½ yards of 108" wide

SAMPLE QUILT
Happy Chance by Laura Heiane for Windham Fabrics and Kona Cotton Solids - Black & Coal by Robert Kaufman Fabrics

QUILTING PATTERN
Wind Swirls

PATTERN
66

Daydreaming Wings

DAYDREAMING WINGS SIZE
18¼" x 17"

PROJECT SUPPLIES
¾ yard of main fabric
¼ yard of accent fabric
½ yard of Heat n Bond Lite
¾ yard of Peltex Single Sided
Fusible Stabilizer
¾ yard of fusible fleece - 20" wide
1 yard of ½" elastic

PATTERN
82

WING TEMPLATES
msqc.co/daydreamingwingstemp

Periwinkle Plates

QUILT SIZE
78½" x 78½"

BLOCK SIZE
14" unfinished, 13½" finished

QUILT TOP
1 package of 10" print squares
1 package of 5" print squares
3¾ yards of background fabric

BORDER
2½ yards

BINDING
¾ yard

BACKING
5 yards - vertical seam(s)
or 2½ yards of 108" wide

OTHER
Missouri Star Small Periwinkle
(Wacky Web) Template for
5" Charm Packs - optional
Missouri Star Mini Periwinkle
(Wacky Web) Template for
2½" Squares - optional
10½ yards of (20" wide)
lightweight fusible interfacing

SAMPLE QUILT
Mint Crush by Lisa Audit
for Wilmington Prints,
Cotton Supreme Solids
- Twilight by RJR Fabrics

QUILTING PATTERN
Little Nature

PATTERN
88

Signature Quilt

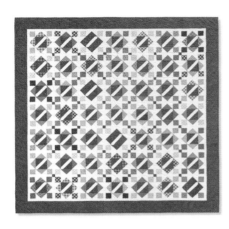

QUILT SIZE
73" x 73"

BLOCK SIZE
8½" unfinished, 8" finished

QUILT TOP
1 roll of 2½" print strips
1 yard of print fabric
  for center squares*
¼ yard of print fabric
  for cornerstones*
3½ yards of background fabric
  - includes sashing & inner border

OUTER BORDER
1¼ yards

BINDING
¾ yard

BACKING
4½ yards - vertical seam(s)
  or 2¼ yards of 108" wide
  print fabric*

OTHER
Missouri Star Marker

*__Note__: We chose to use a print
backing fabric for our center squares,
cornerstones, and quilt backing. If you
chose the same, you will only need
5½ yards or 2¼ yards of 108" wide
print backing.

SAMPLE QUILT
Bee Plaids by Lori Holt
  for Riley Blake Designs

QUILTING PATTERN
Meandering Flowers

PATTERN
98

Stars & Stripes
Table Runner

PROJECT SIZE
52" x 15"

BLOCK SIZE
11½" unfinished, 11" finished

PROJECT TOP
1 package of 2½" solid strips
¼ yard of background fabric

BORDER
½ yard

BINDING
½ yard

BACKING
1 yard - vertical seam(s)

SAMPLE PROJECT
Kona Cotton - Bright Rainbow
  Palette by Robert Kaufman

QUILTING PATTERN
Stars and Loops

PATTERN
104

GENERAL QUILTING

- All seams are ¼" inch unless directions specify differently.
- Cutting instructions are given at the point when cutting is required.
- Precuts are not prewashed, therefore do not prewash other fabrics in the project.
- All strips are cut width of fabric.
- Remove all selvages.

PRESS SEAMS

- Use a steam iron on the cotton setting.
- Press the seam just as it was sewn right sides together. This "sets" the seam.
- With dark fabric on top, lift the dark fabric and press back.
- The seam allowance is pressed toward the dark side. Some patterns may direct otherwise for certain situations.
- Follow pressing arrows in the diagrams when indicated.
- Press toward borders. Pieced borders may need otherwise.
- Press diagonal seams open on binding to reduce bulk.

BORDERS

- Always measure the quilt top 3x before cutting borders.
- Start measuring about 4" in from each side and through the center vertically.
- Take the average of those 3 measurements.
- Cut 2 border strips to that size. Piece strips together if needed.
- Attach 1 to either side of the quilt.
- Position the border fabric on top as you sew. The feed dogs can act like rufflers. Having the border on top will prevent waviness and keep the quilt straight.
- Repeat this process for the top and bottom borders, measuring the width 3 times.
- Include the newly attached side borders in your measurements.
- Press toward the borders.

BINDING

find a video tutorial at: www.msqc.co/006

- Use 2½" strips for binding.
- Sew strips end-to-end into 1 long strip with diagonal seams, aka the plus sign method (next). Press the seams open.
- Fold in half lengthwise, wrong sides together, and press.
- The entire length should equal the outside dimension of the quilt plus 15" - 20."

PLUS SIGN METHOD

find a video tutorial at: www.msqc.co/001

- Lay 1 strip across the other as if to make a plus sign, right sides together.
- Sew from top inside to bottom outside corners crossing the intersections of fabric as you sew.
- Trim excess to ¼" seam allowance.
- Press seam open.

ATTACH BINDING

- Match raw edges of folded binding to the quilt top edge.
- Leave a 10" tail at the beginning.
- Use a ¼" seam allowance.
- Start in the middle of a long straight side.

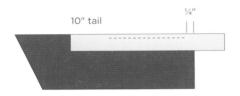

MITER CORNERS

- Stop sewing ¼" before the corner.
- Move the quilt out from under the presser foot.
- Clip the threads.
- Flip the binding up at a 90° angle to the edge just sewn.
- Fold the binding down along the next side to be sewn, aligning raw edges.
- The fold will lie along the edge just completed.
- Begin sewing on the fold.

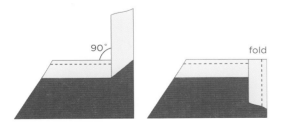

CLOSE BINDING

MSQC recommends The Binding Tool from TQM Products to finish binding perfectly every time.

- Stop sewing when you have 12" left to reach the start.
- Where the binding tails come together, trim the excess leaving only 2½" of overlap.
- It helps to pin or clip the quilt together at the 2 points where the binding starts and stops. This takes the pressure off of the binding tails while you work.
- Use the plus sign method to sew the 2 binding ends together, except this time when making the plus sign, match the edges. Using a pencil, mark your sewing line because you won't be able to see where the corners intersect. Sew across.

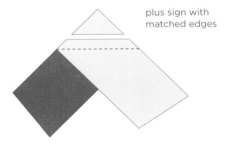

plus sign with matched edges

- Trim off the excess; press the seam open.
- Fold in half wrong sides together, and align all raw edges to the quilt top.
- Sew this last binding section to the quilt. Press.
- Turn the folded edge of the binding around to the back of the quilt and tack into place with an invisible stitch or machine stitch if you wish.